VOLUME 2

Repairing Worn Ball Joints

Minimize the possibility of premature failure

BALL JOINTS, the pivots of the front suspension, are not normally considered a weekend mechanic's service item. It is possible for a weekender to learn to replace the ball joints, but the time required, and the investment in special tools that would be necessary, effectively eliminate the work from the backyard.

However, just because you cannot replace ball joints does not mean you should ignore them until a professional mechanic recommends replacements. A set of ball joints can be a very expensive job and you should know enough about them to minimize the possibility of a premature failure, and be able to check them periodically.

The typical suspension has two ball joints at each wheel, one in the upper control arm, one in the lower, each attached to one end of the steering knuckle. A coil spring or torsion bar (a spring that twists and untwists) and a shock absorber complete the suspension arrangement. If the spring sits on (or in the case of the torsion bar is attached to) a particular control arm, the ball joint at the end of that control arm carries the load for the suspension, and the other ball joint (called the follower) merely keeps the wheel in alignment.

As you might expect, the ball joint that carries the load is the one that normally wears the fastest. This doesn't mean that the follower is immune to wearing out, just that if the load-carrier is good, the follower also is unlikely to need replacement. In any case, you should periodically check the ball joints, both types.

There are several types of ball joints and the method of checking depends both on

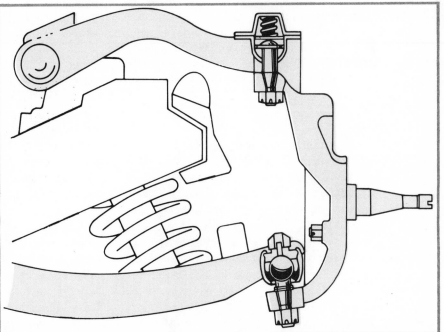

➤ *Typical front suspension. The wheel, not shown, is mounted on the spindle at the right. The part that the spindle attaches to is the steering knuckle. The knuckle has a ball joint at the top and another at the bottom. These join it to the upper and lower control arms. In this design, the lower ball joint is the load-carrying one. Usually, only the load-bearing ball joint receives enough wear to require replacement.*

the design of the joint and whether the upper or lower one is the load-carrier.

If the lower ball joint is the load-carrying one (torsion bar is attached to it or lower part of coil spring sits on it), jack up the side of the car to be checked with the jack under the lower control arm, just under the spring pad or mounting, until the wheel is an inch or two off the ground.

If the upper joint is the load-carrier (coil spring sits on upper control arm), jack up the car under the chassis frame member until the wheel is off the ground.

The jacking of the wheel in the appropriate manner unloads the ball joint, so that any free play you measure in the joint is caused by wear. Now proceed to measure the play.

Slip a pry bar under the tire and place one hand on the top of the tire. With the pry bar, jack up on the tire until any further movement encounters great resistance, that is, you would be trying to jack the entire side of the car up. You now have taken up all play in the ball joint. Release the pry bar and the distance the wheel drops is the play in the joint.

This "feel" method, relying on your hand to estimate the play from the drop of the wheel, may be difficult for a beginner. An alternate method is to use a helper to jack up the wheel and release, while you closely watch the joint and estimate the play.

How much play is acceptable? On this subject there is a fair degree of controversy. On some cars the manufacturers specify a free play of no more than 0.050-inch, while others go as high as 0.200-inch. A reasonable approach is this: if your car does not have the wear indicator-type of ball joint (discussed later), a 0.200-inch limit for one car should be acceptable for another, so if free play seems to be under ¼-inch, the joint is okay for continued service. If it seems to be just over ¼-inch, remove the wheel bearing dust cap, nut cap

and cotter pin, and tighten the wheel bearing nut—finger tight—to remove free play. Then recheck ball joint play, and any play you find you will know is in the ball joint alone.

Also check the follower ball joint. Grab the wheel at the top and bottom and try to move it in and out. If there is more than ¼-inch free play, the follower is worn.

After completing the tests, be sure to reset the wheel bearing nut so that the bearing is just free.

Note: it is a good idea to have a helper try to move the wheel while you watch the follower ball joints, to make sure the wheel movement reflects the play in those ball joints too.

Wear indicator joints. Starting in 1973, General Motors has been gradually changing over its cars to load-carrying joints with wear indicators, so there is no guesswork about whether or not to change the joint. The wear indicator design is not used on the follower joint.

If the wear indicator is flush with the bottom of the joint, so that you can slide the tip of a screwdriver across, the joint is excessively worn. The indicator on a new joint projects only 0.050-inch, so that when it is flush with the bottom of the joint, only that much wear is indicated. However, this test is made with the ball joint loaded (no jacking necessary), and the internal design of the ball joint is such that if 0.050-inch wear takes place, the ball joint is gone.

Maintenance. The ball joint should enjoy a long life, if it is given minimum maintenance, namely proper periodic lubrication. Although some older cars have carried "lubed for life" advertising, the ball joints were fitted with little plugs, so that lubrication could be performed if necessary in so-called "heavy-duty" operation. Heavy-duty translates into driving on anything but smooth-as-silk turnpikes.

If your ball joints are still in serviceable

Repairing Worn Ball Joints

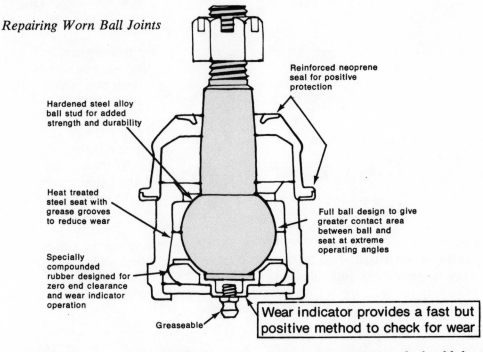

Reinforced neoprene seal for positive protection

Hardened steel alloy ball stud for added strength and durability

Heat treated steel seat with grease grooves to reduce wear

Full ball design to give greater contact area between ball and seat at extreme operating angles

Specially compounded rubber designed for zero end clearance and wear indicator operation

Greaseable

Wear indicator provides a fast but positive method to check for wear

condition, you can begin lubrication immediately and prolong their life.

Remove the plugs with a wrench. You can obtain a special tip for your grease gun to lube directly into the hole. A less expensive procedure is to thread in a grease fitting, which will make lubrication even easier.

Grease gun. The only type of grease gun that should be used on late-model cars is the manual type, for the air-operated type can damage the ball joint grease seals.

The lever handle gun is normally the easiest to operate. In most cases, the gun comes with a 45-degree angle steel injection nozzle, but you will not be able to get it on the upper ball joint fitting. Therefore, buy a flexible nozzle having a pressure rating of at least 4500 p.s.i.

There are many grades of chassis grease, but the best is "moly" grease, which contains 3 to 10 percent molybdenum disulphide, a natural substance that adheres well to metal and has excellent lubricating properties. Even if most of the grease is pounded out of the ball joint, the moly additive will reduce friction and wear.

If temperatures are consistently below freezing during the winter season in your area, the grease used should be labeled "water resistant."

The tip of the grease gun should catch on the nipple of the fitting, so that once it's on it will not slip off. Just push the nozzle straight on with moderate pressure and it will catch. Pump slowly until seals start to swell. You may not be able to see seals swelling, so have a helper wrap a hand around the seal before you start.

Ball joint seals. The grease seals on the ball joints are exposed and may be damaged by road debris (sharp pebbles, etc.). If the ball joints are not worn past tolerances, you can have the seals replaced on the load-carrying joints. The cost of seal replacement is perhaps one-fourth that of new ball joints.

Wheel balancing. You can help reduce some of the shock the ball joints must absorb by keeping the wheels balanced. On-the-car dynamic balancing costs a little more than off-the-car static balance, but it's the only type that balances a spinning wheel on the car, hence it's the only type that really does the job. P.W.

See also: SHOCK ABSORBERS, AUTO; BEARINGS; POWER STEERING, AUTO.

Build a Backyard Barbecue

This simple masonry project can make outdoor cookery convenient as well as fun

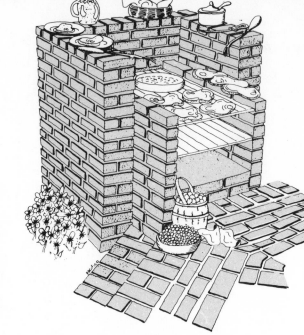

I F LUGGING a sooty portable charcoal broiler with rusty wheels in and out of the garage all summer is a nuisance, why not replace it with a permanent outdoor fireplace.

You can build one of masonry block and concrete easily and economically. Start by laying a foundation.

The foundation is a concrete slab about four inches thick and two inches wider on each side than the fireplace. It extends to about one inch above ground level.

To make the slab, excavate earth, stone or other material to slightly below the surface of the ground. Level and tamp the earth, then place 2 x 4-inch boards to form the edges of the slab, as shown in the diagram. Pour a two-inch layer of concrete into the form, put reinforcing grid or bars in place, then complete pouring.

In poorly drained soil, or in climates where the ground is subject to severe frost heaving, dig a deeper foundation and pour the slab on a four-inch deep layer of gravel or crushed stone.

The fireplace shown in the diagram is built of concrete block and lined with fire brick. These bricks are 9 x 4½ x 2½ inches and four of them cover about one square foot. Lay the brick so that the wide face is exposed to the fire. Use air-setting, high-temperature cement mortar, about 35 pounds for each 100 bricks.

See also: FIREPLACE; OUTDOOR COOKING.

Build a Backyard Barbecue

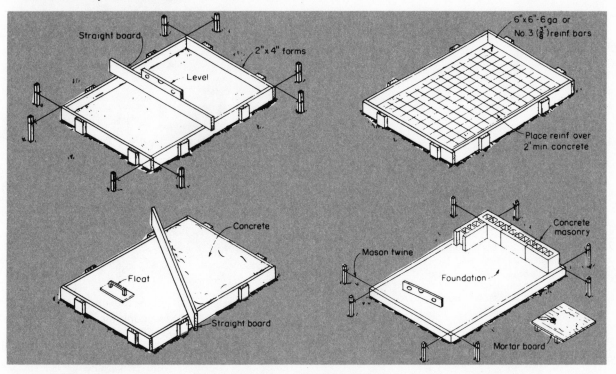

▲ *Forming and construction methods for a simple slab foundation for an outdoor fireplace.*

▼ *Details and cross sections of a typical outdoor fireplace.*

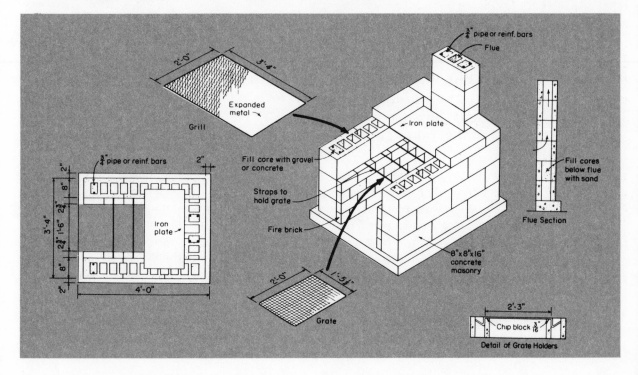

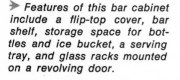

> Features of this bar cabinet include a flip-top cover, bar shelf, storage space for bottles and ice bucket, a serving tray, and glass racks mounted on a revolving door.

Inexpensive Bar Cabinet

There's no finishing involved in building this bar; a prefinished fruitwood panel takes care of that

THIS ATTRACTIVE bar-cabinet features a revolving door with racks for glasses and a detachable front panel which doubles as a serving tray. The use of prefinished panels for all exposed surfaces eliminates the need for finishing and gives the completed piece a professional appearance.

The well-proportioned bar has ample storage space for bottles, glassware, ice bucket and the like. The compartment to the left also has a small shelf near the top which is ideal for storing recipes, stirrers, tongs, etc. This self is placed high enough to clear the bottles stored below it.

To add further to the appearance, prefinished cove molding is used to edge the lid and base, thus solving the problem of what to do with exposed edges. When carefully cut and applied, the molding looks like it was cut from the panel with a shaper or router. Miters must be cut with a sharp blade; otherwise, the wood can splinter resulting in an unsightly appearance.

Care must also be exercised when cutting the panels as the prefinished surface has a degree of brittleness which makes it prone to surface splitting. This is especially apparent when using dull tools. The best blade for a table or radial arm saw when

baseboard: see floors, tiling

working with prefinished panels is a plywood blade. These are hollow ground and cut very smoothly.

Prefinished panels come in a wide variety of styles and woods. Some are solid panels without grooves while others have random grooves and still others have narrow bands or grooves with wide panels between. Prices vary depending upon location and quality. The wood selected and the grain pattern have a direct bearing on

the price, which in any event will be within a modest operating budget.

Use a non-staining white glue for assembling all sections and where necessary, use clamps. Clamping will not be practical when working with the cove molding. Here strips of masking tape are recommended to hold the piece while the glue dries.

Both doors are faced with the prefinished material. A framing of ½-inch pine is sandwiched in between to build up the

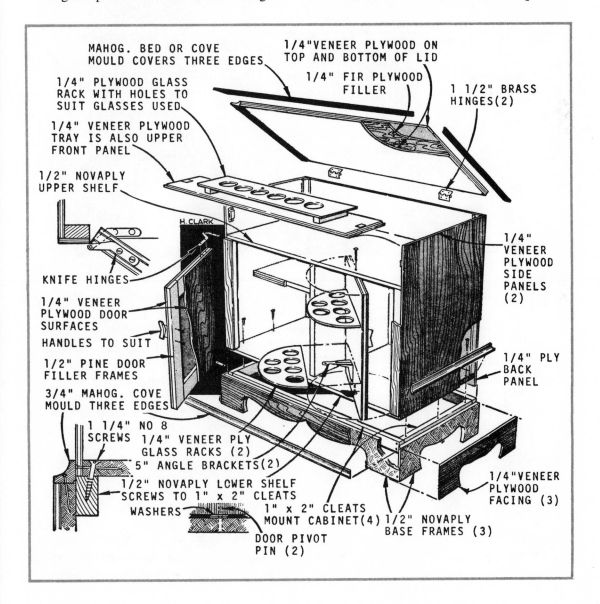

MAHOG. BED OR COVE MOULD COVERS THREE EDGES

1/4" PLYWOOD GLASS RACK WITH HOLES TO SUIT GLASSES USED

1/4" VENEER PLYWOOD TRAY IS ALSO UPPER FRONT PANEL

1/2" NOVAPLY UPPER SHELF

KNIFE HINGES

1/4" VENEER PLYWOOD DOOR SURFACES

HANDLES TO SUIT

1/2" PINE DOOR FILLER FRAMES

3/4" MAHOG. COVE MOULD THREE EDGES

1 1/4" NO 8 SCREWS 1/4" VENEER PLY GLASS RACKS (2)

5" ANGLE BRACKETS(2)

1/2" NOVAPLY LOWER SHELF SCREWS TO 1" x 2" CLEATS

WASHERS

DOOR PIVOT PIN (2)

1" x 2" CLEATS MOUNT CABINET(4)

1/2" NOVAPLY BASE FRAMES (3)

1/4"VENEER PLYWOOD ON TOP AND BOTTOM OF LID

1/4" FIR PLYWOOD FILLER

1 1/2" BRASS HINGES(2)

1/4" VENEER PLYWOOD SIDE PANELS (2)

1/4" PLY BACK PANEL

1/4"VENEER PLYWOOD FACING (3)

H. CLARK

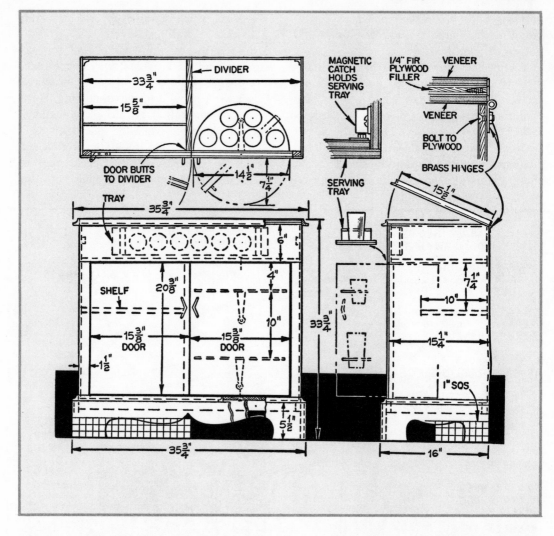

thickness and to prevent warping. The serving tray panel is held in place against the side panels by a friction fit bearing. The overhanging molding on the front edge of the lid also tends to hold the tray panel securely. When the lid is raised the tray may be removed by pulling it forward slightly to overcome the slight side pressure. If desired, a pair of magnetic catches may be added at the ends.

A pair of knife hinges is used to support the swinging door. These are attached at the top and bottom into a recess cut in the door. The revolving door is affixed by means of a pivot that consists of a pair of two-inch nails placed as shown. Two small washers at the bottom will allow the door to revolve freely. When drilling the hole for the pivot in the door, be sure it is straight and square.

The base is made by gluing the prefinished stock to a piece of ½-inch pine. Refer to the drawing as to edge treatment. When your bar-cabinet is completely assembled, break all sharp edges with fine sandpaper, then stain the inside if desired.

See also: FURNITURE, INDOOR; FURNITURE, OUTDOOR.

Inexpensive Bar Cabinet

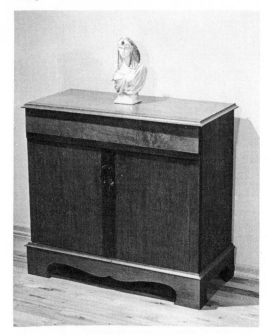

◄ *Panel on front of bar, between doors and lid, converts to a convenient serving tray.* ▲

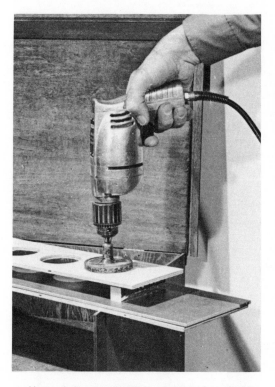

▲ *Use a hole saw to make cutouts for glasses on revolving door racks.*

▲ *Rivet brackets to the revolving door. Then rivet glass trays to the brackets.*

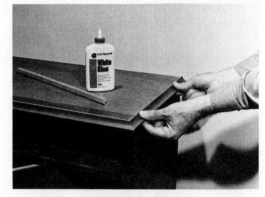

▲*Headed nail serves as pivot for revolving door. It was driven home after photo was taken.*

▲*White glue bonds prefinished molding to cabinet. Use masking tape rather than clamps to hold molding in place while glue dries.*

MATERIALS LIST

Quantity	Size and Description		Purpose
4	$1/4''$	$15^3/8''$x$20^3/8''$ prefinished fruitwood	doors
2	$1/4''$	$1^1/2''$x$20^3/8''$ prefinished fruitwood	end strips
2	$1/4''$	$15^1/4''$x$29^3/8''$ prefinished fruitwood	sides
1	$1/4''$	$5^1/2''$x$35^3/4''$ prefinished fruitwood	outer front base
2	$1/4''$	$5^1/2''$x$15^1/2''$ prefinished fruitwood	outer side base
2	$1/4''$	$15^1/2''$x$34^1/4''$ prefinished fruitwood	lid
2	$1/4''$	$7^1/4''$x$14^1/2''$ prefinished fruitwood	glass rack
1	$1/4''$	$6''$x$34^1/4''$ prefinished fruitwood	outer serving tray
1	$1/4''$	$6''$x$33^3/4''$ prefinished fruitwood	inner serving tray
1	$1/4''$	$15^1/2''$x$34^1/4''$ fir plywood	inner lid
1	$1/4''$	$4^1/2''$x$24''$ fir plywood	serving tray glass rack
1	$1/4''$	$33''$x$34^1/4''$ pine	rear
4	$1/2''$	$2^1/2''$x$20^3/8''$ pine	door frame
4	$1/2''$	$2''$x$11^3/8''$ pine	door frame
1	$1/2''$	$5^1/2''$x$35^1/4''$ pine	inner front base
2	$1/2''$	$5^1/2''$x$15^1/2''$ pine	inner side base
1	$1/2''$	$15''$x$33^3/4''$ Novaply	upper shelf
1	$1/2''$	$15''$x$33^3/4''$ Novaply	lower shelf
1	$3/4''$	$10''$x$16''$ pine	small shelf
1	$3/4''$	$14''$x$20^1/2''$ pine	divider
	$3/4''$	$1^1/4''$x$20^3/8''$ pine	rear end strips
	$1''$	$1''$x$6'$ pine	cleats
2	$2''$ nails and washers		pivot

NOTE: Also need, white glue, hardware and masking tape.

Shaving Bars

Two projects that enable you to keep your shaving equipment together and the bathroom neat

I F YOU FIND your shaving gear cramped for space in the medicine cabinet, build a wall-hung shaving bar. Here are two excellent models styled by a noted industrial designer. Each of these is easily constructed of cabinet wood, aluminum, glass and mosaic tile. An electric glue gun makes bonding these construction

When cementing aluminum to the shaving bar's shelves, heat the metal with glue gun first for a better bond.

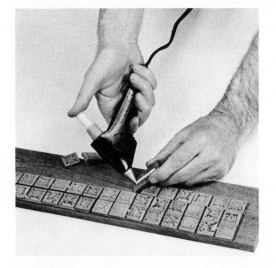

▲ The hot glue also makes fast work of attaching the mosaic tiles to front shelf of this one. Glue sets in just 60 seconds.

▲ There's added storage behind the dropfront shelf or counter of this shaving bar. Little magnet catch keeps it closed.

materials together a cinch; it does the job in one minute flat, without the use of clamps.

One model features a mirror that slides up for access to the interior of the cabinet, and a lower drop-front that doubles as a closure and shelf. This cabinet is made of ½-inch solid walnut, except for the hardboard back and plywood mirror panel. Remember that the side pieces must be mirror images of each other, not exact duplicates.

These are grooved at the rear to take the back panel, and at the front for the sliding mirror unit. Note that a supporting plywood panel, not the mirror itself, slides in the grooves. The mirror is simply cemented to the panel. The panel is rabbeted at the top and bottom for long aluminum angle "irons" that serve as handles, and along the sides to fit into approximately $\frac{9}{16}$-inch wide grooves on the cabinet sides.

The mirror is held in the raised position

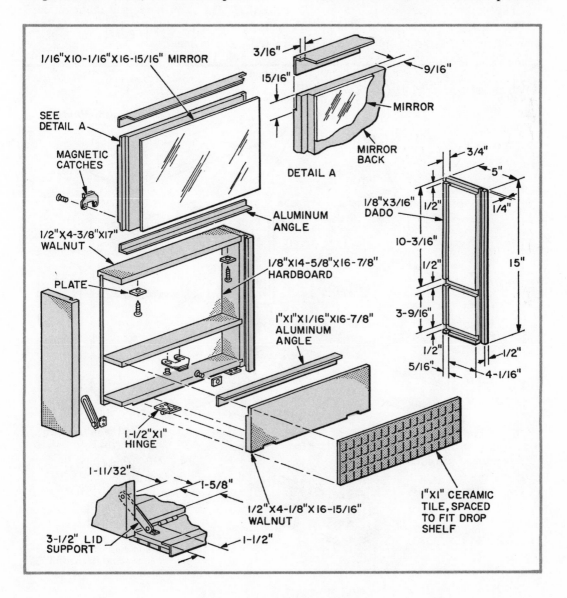

by magnetic catches. Mount these catches onto the mirror backing and fit the mirror unit into place *before* you glue the sides of the cabinet into position.

The hot glue is used to bond the ceramic tile to the drop-front. An aluminum angle across the top provides a handle for this door. Heat the aluminum (and those on the mirror panel) before applying the stick glue. A desk-lid type arm supports the panel in the open position; a magnetic catch keeps it closed.

The other model has a front that swings out. Study the diagrams carefully, and note that the front *nests* over the main part of the cabinet which is made of pine and a hardboard back panel. Retaining edges on the shelves consist of angle-aluminum cemented onto the rabbeted shelf edges.

The swinging front is a three-sided affair with a mirror on the inside. It is made of ½-inch solid walnut and a hardboard back. Metal corner braces are used on the right-hand hinge post for added strength.

The walnut sections are stained and varnished. The front panel and the main cabinet parts are painted.

See also: FURNITURE, INDOOR.

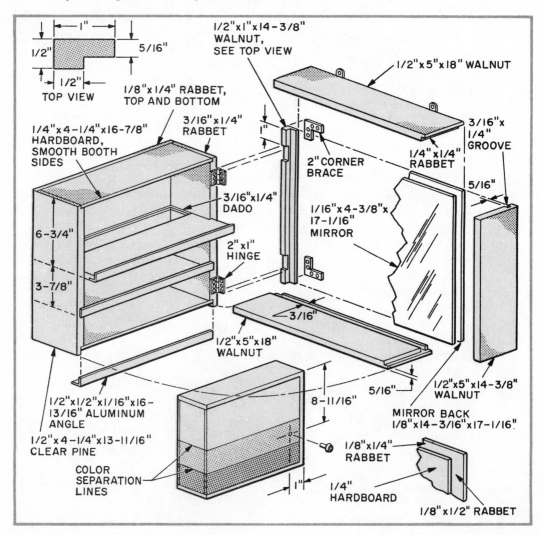

Build This Rustic Bar

Hatchet, torch and wire brush give the common pine lumber of this handsome bar a rustic, weather-beaten look

HERE'S A STRONG, attractive rustic bar suitable for use in a sheltered outdoor location, or in the recreation room indoors. Use of common pine lumber and fir plywood makes it inexpensive to build, and the judicious application of a hatchet, propane torch, and wire brush give it an expensive antique appearance.

Start by making up a box frame, using 2 x 2-inch stock fastened with glue and 16d common nails. Be sure to drill pilot holes for the nails to avoid splitting the wood. Uprights are 35 inches long; in the installation shown the longitudinal members are 62¾ inches long and the cross pieces are 17⅞ inches long in order to take the tile panels that make up the bar top surface. These dimensions can be altered to suit your own needs.

Cut the 4 x 4-inch members to length, and glue and clamp them in place on the frame. Drill the necessary pilot holes and fasten with 2½-inch #8 wood screws. The screws go through the frame members into the 4 x 4s. Add the 4 x 4 cross piece at the top of the uprights, using angled wood braces as shown.

Now use a hatchet or small axe to rough up the edges of the 4 x 4 members. Remember that a sharp tool not only works best, but is safest to use. Scorch the surface of the wood with a propane torch, then give it a good wire brushing.

Add the facing strips and kick plate to the front of the bar and to the sides. Use ¾-inch pine stock in the widths shown; fasten with glue and 6d finishing nails. Install the 1 x 2-inch edging strip across the back of the bar as shown. Note that this strip and the 4 x 4s extend ⅝-inch above the top of the frame. This is to accommodate the thickness of the bar top and tiles. Vary this dimension to suit the bar top material you use. Give the assembly two coats of a clear finish.

Cut the plywood front and side panels to size, and give them the finish of your choice. Then install them to the facing

↑ Start by building a box frame of 2 x 2s. Uprights are 35 inches, longitudinal members 62³/₄ inches and cross pieces 17⁷/₈ inches. Members are joined by nails and glue. Be sure to drill pilot holes for nails so wood won't split.

↑ Note all 4 x 4 pieces in place except corner braces where crosspiece joins uprights.

↑ Glue and clamp the 4 x 4 pieces to the frame and fasten them with 2¹/₂-inch #8 screws through frame into 4 x 4s.

↟ Add the facing strip and kick plate to the front of the bar and to the sides, using ³/₄-inch pine stock to the widths shown in the plans. Install a 1 x 2-inch strip across the back of the bar. Note that the strip and the 4 x 4s extend ⁵/₈-inch above the top of the frame. This is to accommodate the thickness of the bar top and tiles.

↟ Cut plywood front and side panels to fit. Finish them, then install them from the inside of the unit, attaching them with glue and small screws.

↟ For a weathered appearance, rough up the edges of the 4 x 4s with a hatchet or a small axe, scorch the surface of the wood with a propane torch and give the whole structure a wire brushing. Then give it a clear finish.

⩔ If you want casters on your bar, get the heavy-duty type and install them as shown.

◀ *Decorative plates on front panels are made of plastic. They are attached with glue.*

◀ *Cut the top panel to size and attach it with glue and screws. Tiles were embedded in an adhesive. The space between the tiles was filled with grout to form a durable, spill-proof surface.*

▲ *Bent, rusty nail adds a rustic touch to the top cross member.*

strips from inside the unit, using glue and small screws. The decorative panel moldings shown are actually plastic, and they were attached with glue. If casters are to be used, install them as shown.

Finally, cut the top panel to size, and install it with glue and small flat head wood screws. In the installation shown, tile panels were bedded in an adhesive, then spaces between the tiles were filled with tile grout. It's a hard, attractive, and spill-proof surface.

Original design by Steve Ellingson.

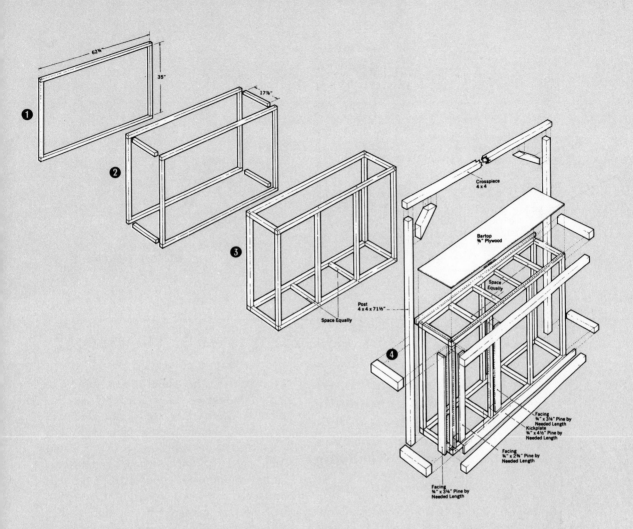

1

62¾"

35"

2

17¾"

3

Space Equally

Post
4 x 4 x 71½"

4

Crosspiece
4 x 4

Bartop
¾" Plywood

Space
Equally

Facing
¾" x 3¼" Pine by
Needed Length
Kickplate
¾" x 4½" Pine by
Needed Length

Facing
¾" x 2¾" Pine by
Needed Length

Facing
¾ " x 3¼" Pine by
Needed Length

MATERIALS LIST		
Quantity	**Size and Description**	**Purpose**
10	2"　　2"x6' fir	framework
6	4"　　4"x6' fire	posts, cross pieces and edging
2	³/₄"　　10"x6' pine	kick plate and facings
1	³/₈"　　4'x8' fire plywood	bar top and panels

NOTE: Also need, glue, angled wood braces, flathead wood screws, 16d common nails, 6d finishing nails, heavy duty casters and decorative bar top.

> *This finished basement is typical of what can be done to transform that dank, lightless hole in the ground beneath your house into enjoyable living space. Major ingredients here are overlaid plywood panels, set out from the dark painted wall on 3/8-inch plywood frames and a floor of asphalt tile. Spiral staircase at left is a space saver.*

How to Take Care of Your Basement

If you've got an unfinished basement that's constantly damp, it can be restored to prime condition — or even finished for living

A DAMP CELLAR is a serious condition for any homeowner, especially when the basement can be converted into useful living space with the aid of attractive modern finishing materials like shag foam carpeting for the floor, wood grain wall panels that are immune to rot, and luminous ceilings that give the recreation room a pleasant daytime brightness. But only a dry basement is suitable for finishing as a family room.

Basement seepage can often be stopped or minimized with an application of waterproofing paint, or if there are leaking spots in the foundation wall, a dose or two of epoxy bonding compound, which is a two-part liquid adhesive that cures within 12 hours to form a permanent seal on poured concrete or cinder block walls.

Of course, a basement that is subject to heavy flooding or sewer problems may require an engineering study and extensive work; less extreme conditions possibly can be handled by installing an automatic sump pump, set into a pit in the basement floor. But the common variety of seepage through cracks in a poured concrete foundation wall, porous cinder blocks, and similar conditions usually are corrected with patching and coatings.

Concrete decks. The basement is a box in the ground. Below grade. The floor is a poured concrete deck or slab that caps or seals the foundation limits (the basement walls are built on the foundation or footings), for its part in keeping water and dampness out.

The earth outside is a different story. Some earth drains water, some earth holds water. Even when you don't see water, it is present as moisture. In addition to this ground water, there is ground pressure, the whole thing combining to close in on the intruder, the basement. Thus the basement elements, especially the concrete deck, must be structurally sound and free of

How to Take Care of Your Basement

faults. Poor construction, aging, earth changes, and nearby water tables can cause cracking, water seepage, moisture and flooding.

When cracks appear on the deck, there is pressure from below. If the cracking is minor, checks itself and does not worsen, the cracks may be treated with a cement patching compound, available in any hardware store. The technique is similar to spackling a plaster wall, and it will effectively plug anything from hairline cracks to moderately wide and deep cracks.

If the original cracks worsen or if new cracks appear after patching the old ones, the entire deck has to be strengthened with a new layer of cement—about two inches reinforced with wire. While this may be a job for a pro, it is possible to do it yourself with care. This new cap will also solve any "dusting" problems you may have had.

Basement walls. Basement walls are built on footings (the deck is poured after the walls are up) and consist these days of cement blocks; older homes will have poured concrete walls. The outer walls are coated with a sealer by the builder, then earth (and, frequently, building construction de-

⋀ *Seeping moisture has caused ordinary paint on this cinderblock basement wall to discolor and peel. Before the wall is resealed with basement paint or an epoxy sealer, the existing paint must be removed completely. This can be done with a wire brush. Oil paint can be burned off with a torch.*

⋀ *Water, water everywhere. Getting your basement reasonably dry and keeping it that way is essential if you intend to refinish it.*

◂ *Baseboard and tile floor show heavy damage from water that has seeped into basement.*

bris) is piled against the outside. Water in time works on these coatings and there are occasional breaks, but the more vulnerable spot is at the base of the wall where water collects in air spaces created by the old debris. Thus leakage will occur at the deck-to-wall joint. It may also build up and stain the lower section of the basement wall.

Recapping the deck, as described earlier, also caps this joint and solves the problem. If the deck is not recapped, the joint can be skinned over or sealed with one of the epoxy sealers, available in cans from the hardware store. There is also a cement curb which can be installed along the floor-to-wall line, but this requires forms which may prove too much a bother. The commercial sealers are good and convenient.

The alternative to this remedy is an enormous project involving the removal of earth from the outside of the house, the removal of the debris at the base of the foundation walls, the drying out of everything, and the recoating of the exterior wall. However, this waterproofing method is absolute. Perhaps it is a vacation project.

Dampness beyond any outright leakage can often be managed by proper ventilation. Humidity can be controlled with a humidifier, eliminating condensation when the warm air hits the cold deck. Exposed

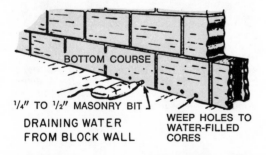

BOTTOM COURSE

1/4″ TO 1/2″ MASONRY BIT

DRAINING WATER
FROM BLOCK WALL

WEEP HOLES TO
WATER-FILLED
CORES

▲ *Sometimes ground water accumulates in the hollow cores of masonry blocks in the lower courses of basement walls. If you're using epoxy sealer, drain the blocks by drilling holes into the cores with a 1/4 to 1/2-inch masonry bit.*

pipes can also be wrapped in felt and taped. Standard basement windows can be replaced with louvers—or one pane in a standard window can be replaced with a silent exhaust fan.

Assuming the basement is unfinished, much can be done to button it up in the way of improvements: finished walls and a tile floor are often all that's needed to make everything watertight.

Walls, for example, require simple stud framing (the air space), followed by an insulation material (such as sheet foam), followed by a vapor barrier (such as builder's paper), followed by the finished paneling. Some of these products come with the insulation and barrier layers bonded to the underside of the paneling; insulation comes with the vapor barrier bonded. Whatever the combination, the total effect is a triple layer that fights dampness, at the same time finishing off an unused or formerly unattractive space. If the basement wall also had asphalt paint on it, then that makes four layers of protection.

Tiling the floor is the equivalent of sealing the deck—and then some. The original cracks should be patched, then the whole deck buttered with bonding cement, followed by 1/8-inch vinyl tiles. That is a good seal.

Routine patching. There are other routine patching jobs. First, inspect all the basement windows, particularly the sealed area between the metal or wooden window frame and the foundation wall. Poke a nail in the area and test for softness, flaking, or crumbled bits. Clean the space thoroughly, dampen it with a sponge, and fill in with fresh mortar mix.

While at the window, also check for hairline cracks starting at the corners of the window installation. Clean and chip, as necessary, and fill these cracks.

Next, examine all of the points on the foundation walls where pipes or conduit enter or leave—the main drains, the water intake line, the natural gas intake line, the conduit for the power lines, the vent or exhaust pipes for the clothes dryer. These are all points of possible water entry and must be thoroughly sealed. So once again chip away old matter and butter the cavity with fresh mix.

Large chunks take a little more care. A hole on the flat will have to be built up in the same way a deep hole in a plaster wall is filled—a little bit at a time, let dry, then add more until it is flush with the surface.

Breaks at inside corners can be treated in the same way. However, missing chunks at outside corners need an extra step. Place a flat board against one side of the outside corner, propping it securely. Then fill the space from the other side. It is not necessary to fill all the way; it is better to do it

▲ *Wash down the wall with a light spray from a garden hose before applying waterproofing basement paint. If you're using an epoxy sealer however, do the opposite. Make sure the wall is dry before you apply it. Wait for several consecutive dry days to pass before doing the job.*

▼ *If using a roller to apply basement wall paint, cut in around ceiling, baseboards and corners with a two-inch brush, then roll paint on remaining area with back and forth strokes. Cross roll for better coverage, and finish by rolling all strokes in the same direction.*

▲ *When applying basement paint with a brush, start at the top and work down in three-foot sections. Work the paint into pits in the block, brushing it back and forth in a scrubbing motion. Use final vertical strokes that blend the paint into previously-coated sections.*

partially, then after it dries, transfer the board to the other side and repeat the technique. Removing the board after the second step, there may still be surface imperfections. These can then be covered with a third application, as with a minor crack.

Ideally, all patches should be sealed with a good sealer or concrete paint (such as asphalt paint). Overlap the patches liberally, spreading the paint onto unaffected wall areas as well as onto the pipe or conduit.

If dampness is minor, resulting only from seepage through a porous wall, waterproofing with a cement bonding paint may do the trick. One coat often will be sufficient, applied with a stiff bristle brush to the wall which has been sprayed lightly with the garden hose. The wall must be unpainted, or all old paint completely removed.

A more drastic solution is to paint the seepage area with a two-part epoxy sealer.

Leaks through cracks or other openings are sealed with epoxy cement. Timing and preparation are all-important to successful application. Surfaces must be absolutely dry. Any previous paint should be scraped and brushed off with a stiff wire brush. Pick a dry day to put on the epoxy, with the temperature above 45 degrees. For quicker setting, 70 degrees is better.

Dry out any wet spots, using a gasoline or butane torch, a photo floodlight, or sun lamp. If there is a persistent leak at any one spot, enlarge the hole a bit with a chisel and plug it with hydraulic cement, which can be used even when there is running water. Hold the cement in place until it has begun to harden.

Applying epoxy sealer. The epoxy comes in small containers for mixing batches small enough to be handled at one time without interruption—the cement hardens in 15 minutes and becomes unworkable. For mixing, open both containers—the resin and the hardener. Pour all the hardener into the resin can, so that there is the correct proportion of both parts, which is an important detail. Stir

▲ *If cement floor is treated with a hardener, it must be scrubbed with a muriatic acid solution. Rinse and let it dry thoroughly before starting to paint.*

▲ *Use ordinary deck paint on stairs. Start from the top and work down. If there is no other exit, paint alternate steps. When these are dry, paint the remaining steps.*

vigorously for two minutes with a clean stick or paint paddle.

Apply with an old paint brush—or buy a cheap 2½ or 3-inch nylon brush, which you can discard after use. Have some lacquer thinner at hand, which is the solvent for the epoxy, for cleaning up afterwards. Brush on in generous amount, covering not only the immediate area of

How to Take Care of Your Basement

the leak, but also about a foot beyond the margin. Hairline cracks that are too narrow to chisel should be given a generous coat of epoxy to form a surface seal.

You can apply a second coat if desired to reinforce the coating. However, if water returns before the epoxy sets, it will poke holes through the soft coating; in that event, wait until the area has completely dried, then put on a new coat of sealer. The epoxy dries to a shiny amber color, and may be painted with either epoxy or latex paint.

A final word about permanent flooding problems. Many homeowners have to live with periodic basement flooding whenever there is a heavy downpour. Their houses are situated on ground that promotes this condition despite efforts to keep things dry. A sump pump is a practical answer: basically a hole in the basement floor that collects water, then pumps it out of the house. Things are still damp, but they're not flooded.

▲ *Unlike ordinary basement paint, epoxy sealer requires a dry surface rather than a damp one for application. It's best to wait for a few consecutive dry days before starting to paint. Spots that are still damp can be dried by the flame of a torch.*

▼ *One method of handling water seepage is to install a pump, especially in areas where cellar flooding is common after heavy rains. The pump is installed in a sump cut in the basement floor. It operates automatically as water flows into the sump.*

> Styrofoam insulation is applied board-by-board from the floor up. The board at the top was cut with a knife to fit around window. Warning: don't make any assumptions about the dimensions of your basement. The odds are that nothing will be exactly square, so always measure first, then cut the board and try it in place before putting on the mastic. Note how joints of boards are staggered.

A New Way
to Insulate Your Basement

Insulating boards attach directly to basement walls, allowing installation of finished paneling of your choice

ONE EASY WAY to convert a rough uncomfortable basement into a snug, attractive place for work or play is to panel it, using Styrofoam insulating boards as an undersurface.

The boards are extremely light and easy to handle. They can be cut to fit around windows or doors with an ordinary knife and are attached to the wall with mastic. No nailing is necessary.

In addition to insulating your basement, the Styrofoam also provides a smooth, uniform surface to which any of the widely available wood paneling sheets can be attached with adhesive.

The boards of Styrofoam are laid lengthwise, starting from the floor, with the joints staggered, like giant bricks. Lay one board at a time, cutting it to fit if necessary. Try it in place, then bead it with mastic and simply push it into place on the wall.

One caution. If you plan to hang shelves, bookcases or heavy lamps, etc., from the wall, provide each with a nailing strip. A nailing strip is a piece of wood of appropriate size attached to the wall with mastic and a few concrete nails. It should be the same depth as the Styrofoam. Cut the Styrofoam to fit around it. After the paneling is applied, attach the shelf or lamp through the paneling to the nailing strip beneath.

Also extend electrical outlets and fixtures to bring them flush with the new surface.

Once the Styrofoam boards are in place, the paneling of your choice is applied directly to the surface in much the same manner, except that the paneling is applied vertically rather than horizontally. Each panel is fitted, checked in position, then applied to the surface with mastic.

A New Way to Insulate Your Basement

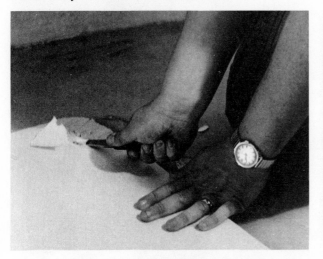

⬆ *What to do about irregularities. It's simple. If something projects slightly from the wall, just use a knife to carve out a hollow for it in the reverse side of the Styrofoam. The right side will still present a smooth surface for paneling.*

⬆ *Once a section of Styrofoam has been checked in its position on the wall, apply Dow #11 mastic using a standard caulking gun with ¹/₄-inch bead and push the board into place. Lay boards lengthwise, starting from floor.*

⬇ *Paneling is applied in about the same way as Styrofoam boards. Rule number one is still: measure first. Apply paneling vertically and be sure it's plumb. Check each sheet in place without mastic. Use a level and mark a line on wall for panel edge when it is applied.*

⬇ *When you are ready to stick the panel to the wall, apply the same mastic you used for the Styrofoam, using the same caulking gun. Apply a bead running around the panel near the edge and a series of Xs as shown in the photo. Note the Styrofoam insulated wall in the background.*

⬆ After you have applied the mastic to the back of the panel, push it into place on the wall, using the mark you have made as a guide for its position. Note the shims on the floor. These are wedged beneath the panel to hold it in a precisely vertical position.

⬆ Rapidly pushing and pulling the panel against the Styrofoam wall will create a quick tacky bond; but be careful. If you fan up too much air pressure, it may blow some of the mastic out to the side. The mastic is difficult to remove. If it gets on a panel, try naphtha or mineral spirits.

⬇ Wood shims wedged between the bottom of the panel and the floor hold the panel in true plumb while the mastic sets.

⬇ The molding used to finish corner and ceiling joints can be attached with glue. An alternative method for completing the ceiling joint is to attach a nailing strip to the wall above the insulation and nail the molding to that.

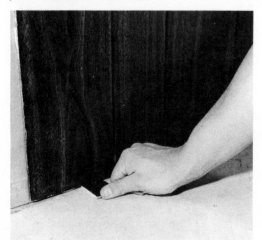

Tying Flies
and Bass Bugs

Try casting for bass or trout with lures you've made yourself

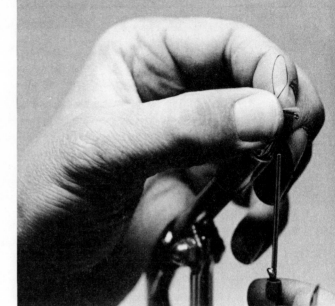

▲ *Tying in tail of Golden Pheasant tippet on the Royal Coachman. Note how thread goes up between thumb and hook, loosely over the tail material and down between the hook and forefinger before it is pulled tight.*

SINCE ANTIQUITY anglers have lured fish with artificial flies and bugs. Many fishermen make their own lures for the thrill of catching a fish on a product of their own hands as well as economy.

The basic procedures in fly tying are easily mastered by most fishermen, and with a little practice you should be able to turn out some fine looking flies. Here, we'll outline the steps in making two of the most popular flies—a Royal Coachman dry fly and a deer hair mouse bass bug. By following the same basic tying procedures and altering the materials used many different patterns can be made.

Basic tools needed are a vise, hackle pliers, small sharp pointed scissors, a bobbin for holding tying thread and a bodkin (dubbing needle). These tools, if of good quality, will cost about $18 with the vise being the biggest expense at about $9. If you want a more elaborate outfit you can add a whip finishing tool, hackle guards, tweezers and a really first class vise for about $10 more.

Materials used in fly tying are infinite in variety ranging from polar bear hair and feathers from Asian birds to scraps of yarn and even fur from your dog or cat. For starters you'll want hooks, various shades of neck hackles (feathers) from game cocks, duck wing and flank feathers, Golden Pheasant tippet feathers, floss and chenille in different colors, herl from the eyed feather of a peacock, deer hair, buck or calf tails, tying thread (prewaxed nylon) and fly tying head cement. These materials as well as books on fly tying can be obtained at most sports and tackle stores. You can also order from the mail order houses specializing in fishing gear. These firms offer catalogs and ordinarily provide fast, reliable service.

When getting started in fly tying it's best to concentrate on simple patterns in the larger sizes until you are adept at the basic procedures. It's also wise to stay with a proved pattern until you have it mastered before trying to make your own "Super Bug Special".

To tie the Royal Coachman dry fly select a No. 10 fine wire dry fly hook and clamp it in your vise with the shank horizontal. If you are right-handed the eye of the hook should point to the right; if left-handed, the opposite. The following instructions are for a right-handed person. If you are left-handed, just switch hands from the way the instructions read.

With your spool of thread held in the bobbin, secure the thread just behind the eye of the hook by laying the loose end along the shank and wrapping over it with the working portion of the thread. After making three or four wraps the thread will be securely fastened to the hook and you can release the loose end. Continue to wind the thread in a tight spiral to the rear until the forward ⅔ of the shank is covered. Then snip off the tag end.

For the tail, select six or eight Golden Pheasant tippet fibers, hold them between your left thumb and forefinger on top of the hook with the natural ends extending past the hook; bend an amount equal to

the length of the hook shank. Bring the thread up between your thumb and the hook, loosely over the tail and down between your forefinger and the hook. Still holding the tail firmly in place pull the thread straight down binding the tail to the hook. Repeat this step twice then slip your left hand to the rear grasping the tail near the tip to hold it in position as you continue to wrap the thread tightly back to the point where the hook starts to bend. Holding the tail as you wrap back insures it will stay in place rather than rolling to the side of the hook.

The body is made in three equal segments, a butt of peacock herl, a center joint of red floss and a shoulder of peacock herl. Tie in a peacock herl at the base of the tail; advance your thread and wind the herl forward three or four wraps. Secure the herl with two wraps of thread and tie in a piece of red floss, advance the thread again. Then wrap the floss smoothly forward for the center third of the body. Secure the floss with a couple of tight wraps of thread, cut off the excess and wrap the shoulder of peacock herl. At this point you should have ³⁄₁₆ to ¼-inch behind the eye of the hook bare except for your initial

▼ *Applying body of peacock herl and red floss. Note the length of the tail and the size of each of the body segments.*

▼ *White duck primary feather wing held in position before tying in. Tips of feathers point up and wing is slightly longer than the body.*

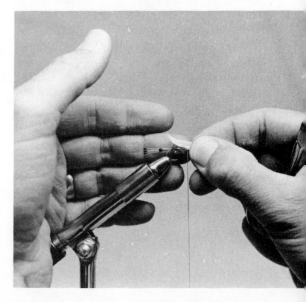

Tying Flies and Bass Bugs

◄ *Hackles are tied in just ahead of body after the wing is secured and pulled upright.*

▼ *Hackles are wound one at a time. Take equal number of turns ahead and behind wing.*

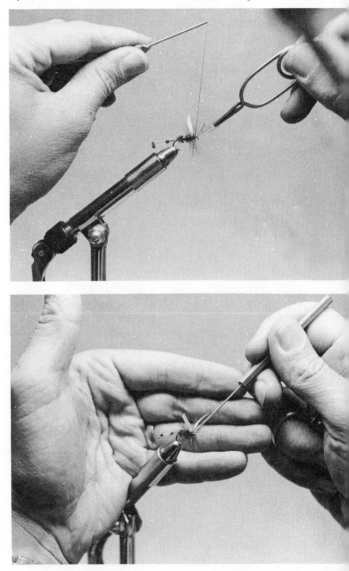

▲ *Apply cement to the head with bodkin. Note the angle at which the wings are splayed out.*

thread wraps. Advance your thread to the center of this area in preparation for tying in the wing.

The standard Royal Coachman wing material is white duck primary flight feathers. From a matched pair of these feathers (two feathers similar in color, shape, size and texture; one from the right wing and one from the left) cut one section about $\frac{3}{16}$-inch wide from each feather. Place the two sections together with the convex sides facing and the tips even. Place the wing on top of the hook with the tips pointed up and extending about $\frac{1}{32}$-inch beyond the body. Holding the wing between your left thumb and forefinger, bring the thread up between the hook and your thumb, loosely over the wing and down between the hook and your forefinger. Now pull the thread straight down relaxing your grip just enough to let the wing compress onto the hook as the thread comes tight. Repeat this step twice, let go of the wing with your left hand and cut away the excess wing material extending forward. Grip the wing near the tip with your right thumb and forefinger and pull it forward into an upright position. Then make several turns of thread behind the wing to hold it upright.

Select two dark brown cock hackles of dry fly quality, place them together with the shiny sides facing and strip off all the fuzz and web at the base of the feathers.

⇒ Start body of the Deer Hair Mouse by making two loose turns of thread around hook and clump of deer hair. Then, pull thread tight causing hair to flare around hook.

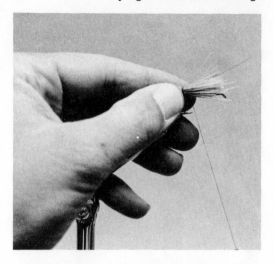

Tie in the hackle stems just forward of the body with the feather portion extending to the rear of the fly. Advance your thread to about $\frac{1}{16}$-inch behind the eye and clip off excess hackle stems. Selecting hackles of the proper size is critical in making a well porportioned fly. On dries the individual barbules of feather should be as long as $1\frac{1}{2}$ times the gap of the hook (distance from point to shank). Grip one of the hackles near the tip with your hackle pliers and wind it forward taking about three turns behind the wing and three in front. As you wrap the hackle, keep it on edge so the individual barbules radiate out perpendicular to the hook shank. Secure the first hackle with a couple turns of thread, wind the second one forward in the same manner, tie it down and cut off the tips. Build a neat head with the tying thread, tie off the thread with two half hitches or better yet a whip finish and cut away the thread. Using your bodkin, separate the wings so they splay out at about a 30° angle from the hook, put a drop of head cement between the wings and on the head. Now sit back and admire your handiwork.

Bass bugs represent large insects, frogs or small animals that have somehow found their way to the surface of a pond or stream. The best material for bugs is deer, antelope or caribou hair in natural or dyed colors. As the body hair is hollow it is very buoyant for good flotation and it also compresses slightly when the bass strikes. This compression gives the fish a natural feel and he'll hang on longer before he detects the fraud, giving you more time to drive the hook home.

To tie deer hair mouse, clamp a long shank No. 6 hook in your vise. Attach stout nylon tying thread at the hook bend and tie in a tail about $1\frac{1}{2}$ inches long of natural gray/brown bucktail. The body is made by "spinning" the deer body hair around the hook, so leave as much of the shank bare of thread as possible because the hair spins best on a bare hook.

From a patch of natural gray/brown deer hair, cut a clump about the diameter of a lead pencil. Strip out all the short hairs and fuzz found near the base of the clump and hold the clump on top of the hook at the bend. Take two loose turns of thread around the clump and the hook, then start to pull the thread tight. As you tighten the thread relax your grip on the hair enough to let it roll all around the hook. As the thread tightens and the hair rotates it will flare out perpendicular to the hook shank. When the thread is tight advance it to the bare shank just past your spun clump and push the clump firmly to the rear. Continue to spin clumps of hair along the hook pushing each clump firmly into the previous one as a tightly packed body is essential for good flotation and durability.

When the hook is completely covered with spun hair and looking like an un-

▲ *First clump of hair after spinning. Be sure hair spins completely around the hook.*

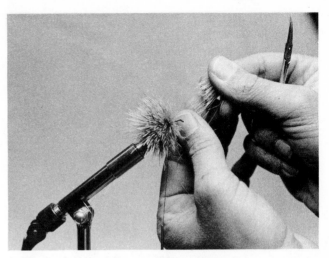

▲ *Short hairs and fuzz must be removed from each clump of hair if it is to spin well.*

▲ *Push each clump back into the previous clumps to insure a tightly packed, bouyant body.*

▲ *Shaping the bug with scissors. Next step is to fish with it.*

kempt bottle brush, tie off the thread and remove the bug from the vise. Using your scissors, carefully trim the bug into the shape of a mouse, leaving a few long hairs for the legs and ears. As a finishing touch you can paint in eyes with black enamel.

Fly tying may seem complicated at first glance but it's really not and with a little persistence in mastering the basic steps is really quite simple. Give it a try and you'll soon be solidly hooked on this fascinating hobby.   **G.B.**

See also: FISHING; TROLLING TECHNIQUES.

Ceramic Tiling Your Bathroom

By doing-it-yourself and using new adhesive cements you can install real ceramic tiles in an average bathroom for a reasonable cost

ONE OF THE FIRST items a proud home owner is likely to mention about his house is the ceramic tile bath, because real ceramic tile in the bathroom or kitchen adds a touch of practical luxury. "Real" (meaning ceramic) tile has a rich, handsome look and, with proper care, it will last the life of a house because its glazed surface resists water, most cleaners and wear.

A new adhesive method makes setting ceramic tile as easy as applying many of the substitute materials that have become popular during the last few years. Of course, ceramic tile materials (Fig. 3C) cost more than some other materials, but the amateur can now obtain them easily, and doing his own setting will offset this higher cost. For comparison, let's consider the simple 5x6-foot bath shown in Fig. 3A. The 87 square feet of tile required to cover the walls only plus the bull nose

cap, feature strip and bottom course would cost about $95. Covering a similar area with plastic tile along with a trim strip around the bottom would cost $51, but considerably more if you pay to have the work done. Making a sketch similar to the one in Fig. 3B will not only allow you to figure what the cost of tiling your bathroom will be, but will help to plan what kind and how many tiles to order.

Field tiles along with the trim pieces (Fig. 3C) are available in a variety of colors along with white and black. Most wall tile is glazed, while floor tile is unglazed to prevent slipping. Sizes of tile vary with the manufacturer, even though standards call for field tile to be 4¼ x 4¼ inches. So buy all of your tile from the same manufacturer and specify a cushion edge—the kind with a slight slope near each edge.

Tiles come in two grades too—standard

and seconds. Standard grade is graded uniformly for color and is free from defects or uneven glazing. The lower-cost seconds may vary in color shade and come with chipped corners or spotty glazing. If you use seconds, buy about 10% more than you need to allow for replacing poor tiles.

Each grade of tile carries three designations: color (specified by number), size (specified by a letter), and shade of color (again specified by number). Most manufacturers stamp these designations on the top of a tile carton, for example, 104-D-5. Make sure all cartons purchased bear identical designations for color match. Colored tiles usually do not cost any more than whites. Wall tiles are usually ⅜-inch thick and come packed in cartons that weigh about 55 pounds each and contain 120 tiles or enough to cover 15 square feet.

Telephoning local tile dealers or installers will usually turn up one who will sell you enough tile to cover a bathroom or kitchen. If you can't buy tile and adhesive locally, order them by low-cost freight from mail order companies.

The two types of adhesive for applying wall tiles are—(1) *buttering wall type,* a quick-setting adhesive that sets in about five minutes after placing on the back of

▼ Spread floating type adhesive with notched trowel. This type of adhesive may be used after the starting course of tile has been set with buttering adhesive, applied with a putty knife.

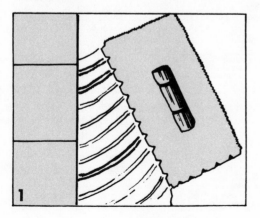

the wall tile, and allows you to do all the starting courses on wall areas of less than 50 square feet without waiting for the adhesive to set up, and (2) *floating wall type* that sets in about one hour and is spread on the wall; you will need both the floating and buttering wall types for wall areas over 50 square feet. Each type covers about 50 square feet per gallon. Adhesives should bear the label "CS-181" to indicate that they meet specified performance requirements. For repairing tile, use the buttering type adhesive.

Making cutouts. The cutter (Figs. 4 and 5) not only cuts wall tile to width, but can also cut tiles on the bias, and split tiles to make cutouts for clearing pipes, and electrical switches. Nippers (Fig. 6) are used to cut off about ⅛-inch piece of tile at a time, working from each end toward the center gradually. Nip off only small pieces, since applying excessive

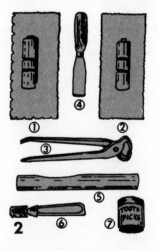

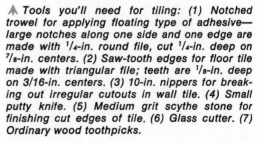

▲ Tools you'll need for tiling: (1) Notched trowel for applying floating type of adhesive— large notches along one side and one edge are made with ¼-in. round file, cut ¼-in. deep on ⅞-in. centers. (2) Saw-tooth edges for floor tile made with triangular file; teeth are ⅛-in. deep on 3/16-in. centers. (3) 10-in. nippers for breaking out irregular cutouts in wall tile. (4) Small putty knife. (5) Medium grit scythe stone for finishing cut edges of tile. (6) Glass cutter. (7) Ordinary wood toothpicks.

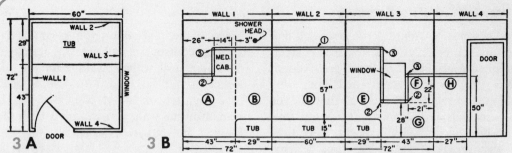

3 A

3 B

3 C

(A) Typical floor plan of bathroom. (B) Layout to scale of bathroom walls in clockwise direction to figure tile quantities and provide working drawings. (C) Types of tile—(1) surface type bull-nose cap; (2) inside corner; (3) creased outside corner; (4) wall field tile; and (5) decorative or feature strip.

Estimating Tile Requirements

The amount of the wall tile required is determined by the height to which you want your wall tile to extend on the walls and the size of your bathroom or powder room walls. The normal height for wall tile in a bathroom is 52 in. except around the shower head area, where it should extend to just below the shower head, or about 72 in.

Let's use a typical 5 x 6-ft. bathroom (Fig. 3A) to show how you can figure the amounts of the wall tile and trim pieces you'll need. Fig. 3B shows the four walls of the bathroom in clockwise rotation with the wall areas divided into convenient rectangles for easy calculation. The corner letters on the cap course are the same as those listed under Fig. 3C. A convenient way to lay out your own plan to scale is to use graph paper.

Tables A and B show quantities required after making a 5% allowance for waste.

Making a similar sketch of your own bathroom or powder room not only helps to find the material required, but also gives you a working drawing. Heights of the wall tile are approximate because the final height will be determined by the actual size of the tile purchased plus the joint spaces. Measuring the distances along walls accurately to the nearest inch is all that is required for estimating purposes.

Table C allows you to easily find out the number of cartons of tile or the number of square feet of wall tile to order, once you have figured out the area of the walls to be tiled in square inches. Just find the wall space figure nearest to that of your own, using the next higher figure in Table C.

Buy your accessories (soap dish, towel bar, etc.) when ordering the ceramic tile so that it is possible to determine sizes of wall cutouts required and location of accessories.

TABLE A—WALL TILE REQUIRED

	Area	Sq. In.
"A"	50 x 43	2150
"B"	57 x 29	1653
"C"	22 x 3	66
"D"	57 x 60	3420
"E"	57 x 29	1653
"F"	22 x 21	462
"G"	43 x 28	1204
"H"	50 x 27	1350

Total 11958 sq. in.
add 5% allowance 600 sq. in.

12558 sq. in.
divided by 144 87 sq. ft.

If carton contains 15 sq. ft. of tile, this area requires six cartons of wall tile.

TABLE B—STRIP TILES REQUIRED

Bull Nose Cap 6" long (Buy S-4200 surface type of cap)	lengths starting at area "A" 24, 20, 46, 60, 29, 42, 18, 20, 21, 27 Total—307 in. divided by 6"—52 pieces allow for breakage— 4 pieces Total to order 56 pieces
Feature Strip 6" long	total length approximately the same as the bull nose cap, so 56 pieces will be required
Bottom Course Wall Tile (If desired in different color)	lengths starting at area "A" 43, 43, 27 Total—113" divided by 4"—29 pieces allow for breakage— 3 pieces Total to order 32 pieces

TABLE C—TILE ORDERING DATA

*Wall Space, Sq. In.	Boxes of Tile Required	Square Feet	Tiles
2050	1	15	120
3080	1½	22½	180
4100	2	30	240
5140	2½	37½	300
6170	3	45	360
7240	3½	52½	420
8220	4	60	480
9250	4½	67½	540
10280	5	75	600
11300	5½	82½	660
12340	6	90	720
13370	6½	97½	780
14400	7	105	840
15400	7½	112½	900
16450	8	120	960

*Allowance of 5% has been made for the waste and breakage. Find actual wall space as shown, and order next higher figure in column #1.

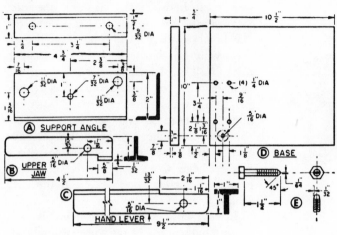

4

5

▲ To make your own tile splitter, saw and file out parts from steel. Bolt support angles (A) to wood base with ¹/₄-in. carriage bolts. A 5/16 x 1-in. machine bolt forms pivot for upper jaw of cutter (B) and this jaw is controlled by the handle (C) also pivoted on a 5/16 x ³/₄-in. machine bolt. A pointed 5/16 x 1¹/₂-in. machine bolt is assembled in line with the center of the upper jaw with its height adjusted by inserting plain washers between its head and the counterbored hole in the base. Allow about 1/16-in. clearance between upper jaw and bolt point when wall tile is in position. The 3/16-in. bolt fastened through the support angles keeps the upper jaw from falling down too low between the angles.

Mount cutter on wood base large enough to fit a trysquare between two ¹/₂-in. strips. Edge of square guides glass cutter when scribing tile. A section of dime-store ruler under the square speeds cutting.

▲ Cutting tile with the splitter is a 2-part operation. Slip tile in position and locate cut from ruler. Scribe tile with glass cutter, bearing down heavily, in one continuous line. Scribe line only once. Insert tile between upper jaw and pointed bolt with scribed line on top and in line with point. Applying pressure on hand lever forces tile apart on line. Minimum width that can be cut is about ³/₄-in.

pressure will crack the tile. Practice this on scrap tiles first.

To make a cutout for a pipe, measure its diameter first. From the course of tile below the pipe measure to the bottom of the pipe and add one half of the pipe diameter. Lay out distance to pipe's center line on a tile. Repeat from the side tile next to the pipe. From pipe's center draw a circle about ¼-inch larger than the pipe diameter (Fig. 7B).

Using the cutter, split the tile vertically

through the center of the circle. With the nippers, cut a semi-circular opening in each half of the split tile to fit around the pipe (Fig. 7A). Use the same procedure for making cutouts to clear electrical switches and receptacles (Fig. 8). In remodeling work, raise the switch or receptacle with spacers under its mounting ears to compensate for the added thickness of tile.

To fit a piece of tile to an irregular edge, such as around the curved edge of the tub (Fig. 9), first cut a cardboard template by trial and error. Then cut a tile to match the template using the cutter and end nippers. The scythe stone (Fig. 2) smooths the edge after the rough outline

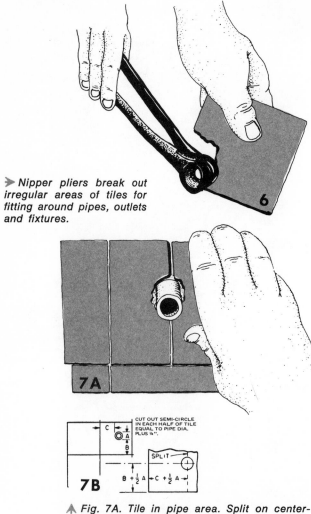

> Nipper pliers break out irregular areas of tiles for fitting around pipes, outlets and fixtures.

7 A

7 B

CUT OUT SEMI-CIRCLE
IN EACH HALF OF TILE
EQUAL TO PIPE DIA.
PLUS ¼".

C

A

B

SPLIT

B + ½ A | C + ½ A

Fig. 7A. Tile in pipe area. Split on center-line. Nippers break out tile in small pieces until it clears pipe. Fig. 7B. Measure from tiles around pipe area to locate cutout to clear pipe. Split tile vertically.

Ceramic Tiling Your Bathroom

has been cut with the nippers. Caulk any space left between the tile and the tub.

Preparing the surface. Ceramic wall tile can be set over plaster, concrete and gypsum wall board at least ½ to ⅜-inch thick if all cracks are repaired and surface is level and free from loose or calcimine paint. If walls have sharp hollows or bumps, spread a coat of underlayment (sold by tile dealers) using a straight edge trowel, and check resulting surface with a straight edge. Cover walls with waterproof primer or shellac (don't prime floors with shellac).

In new work where plasterboard is used in the bathroom, install one of the four paper-bound edges of plasterboard at the intersection with the tub ledge. Heavily prime all edges of wallboard around the tub with the waterproof primer.

In fitting tile around the tub (Fig. 10), note that the vertical edge of the tub lip is set into notches cut into the studs, to present a level surface for the wallboard and the tile. You can leave plumbing fixtures in place and cut and fit the tile around them. However, it's better to remove the fixtures and lengthen all pipe nipples for the lavatory and closet by ½-inch to allow for the thickness of tile and adhesive.

Bathroom accessories. The tile dealer can supply the accessories you need in sets or singly, to match your tile. One type of accessory has a flange which mounts flush with the tile wall. Another type has a flange that overlaps adjoining tiles. If possible, select accessories that will mount in a 4¼x4¼-inch opening, so that you can skip one tile space for the accessory and keep on tiling. For the soap dish and grab bar, you may have to leave out two tiles. Towel bar brackets which require a smaller

Tile can be split along bottom edge of cutout for switch and side pieces split for quicker fitting. Nip out section from one edge of bull nose cap to leave top edge unbroken.

Ceramic Tiling Your Bathroom

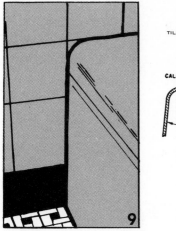

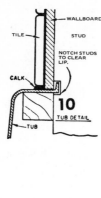

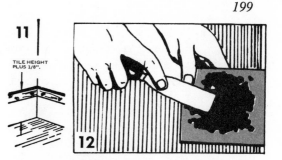

Fig. 11. Straightedged wood strip aligns second course where floor is not level. Lower course cut to fit floor. Fig. 12. Buttering type of adhesive is applied directly to tile to cover about half of area 1/16-in. thick.

Fig. 9. When fitting tiles around irregular areas, such as a bathtub, cut a cardboard template first, break out tile to rough outline with nippers, then smooth with stone. Fig. 10. Around tub's edge, notch studs for lip. Set wallboard and tile close to tub and caulk immediately.

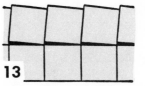

Fig. 13. How corners of tiles not set square project above adjacent tiles. Fig. 14. If you can't get the "lug" type tile (which spaces the tiles automatically) you will have to use toothpicks on all four sides to space the tiles. ▼

opening, should also have the tiles left off the wall where they are to be mounted. Plan the cutouts for the towel rack bar to come in the corner of the tiles, so the flange on the bracket covers the cutouts in the tile.

Cutouts in the wall itself for accessories are made after all of the tiles have been set in place. *Caution*—Mark the location of all wall studs on the wall above the top course of tile so that you don't select a place for your accessory on front of the stud.

Setting wall tile. Now let's get at the job of setting the wall tile. In a remodeling job, remove the baseboard. If you plan to tile the floor (we will explain how to do this after we finish the walls) the base you will need for the floor tile should be in place before starting the wall tiling. Ceramic floor tile can be set on either a concrete base or by covering existing sub-floor with ½-inch exterior grade plywood, nailed to the sub-floor with 1¼-inch screw-type nails. Space nails not over 4 inches apart each way.

Make sure that the floor surface is level.

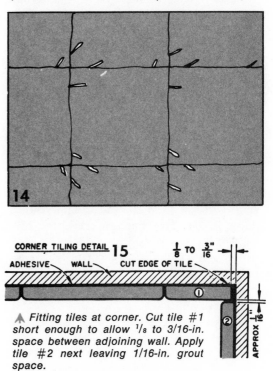

Fitting tiles at corner. Cut tile #1 short enough to allow ⅛ to 3/16-in. space between adjoining wall. Apply tile #2 next leaving 1/16-in. grout space.

If the floor is level within $\frac{3}{16}$-inch or less, go ahead with tiling, starting with the lowest or bottom course. The $\frac{1}{4}$-inch ceramic floor tile covers any space left between the bottom edge of the tile and the floor. Using a level, draw a line on the wall even with the top of a tile placed on the high side of the floor. This will be the top edge of the tile in the lowest course.

If the floor surface is off level by more than $\frac{3}{16}$-inch, nail a straight piece of $\frac{1}{2}$ x 1-inch wood trim to each wall (Fig. 11). Starting at the low end of the lowest wall, measure up the distance equal to one tile plus $\frac{1}{8}$-inch, and draw a line with the level. Nail the wooden strips so their top surfaces are even with this line. Don't drive the nails flush, as the strips will be removed later. The starting course of tile sits on top of these wooden strips. When the rest of the tiling is finished, remove these strips and cut each tile with the nippers or cutter to within $\frac{1}{8}$-inch of the height along the floor course of tile. Use the buttering type of adhesive on the back of tiles set along the bottom, and set the tile with the cut edge down. *Provide good ventilation and avoid smoking when using the solvent-type adhesives.*

If you don't plan to use ceramic floor tile, cement a synthetic rubber cove strip over the joint between the wall tile and the floor covering.

If there is a bathtub in the room you're tiling, start a full course of tile directly over bathtub's ledge. Run one vertical course of tile from this horizontal course down to the base line, which is the top edge of the lowest course of tile. The second course of tile may be cut in height as in Fig. 9.

Before starting, find out how much the end tiles will have to be cut. Lay one course of tile on the floor next to the wall to be tiled, with a toothpick between each tile. Measure the amount of space left for the last tile; if it is $\frac{3}{4}$-inch or less, cut an inch off the starting tile. This short starting tile avoids narrow and difficult-to-cut last tiles. After tiling one wall, measure the tile space on it equal to the next wall, and thus determine if the end tiles for that wall need to be cut.

Starting with the buttering type of adhesive, spread a small amount of it with the putty knife on the back of each tile to cover about half of its surface $\frac{1}{16}$-inch thick (Fig. 12). Immediately press the tile in place on the wall. Draw horizontal lines on the wall surface, one for each course of tile. You must set the tiles square as well as level, or their corners will project as in Fig. 13.

As each tile is added in the horizontal course, place the toothpicks (unless you use the "lug" type tile) on four sides of each tile (Fig. 14) to automatically gage the separation between the tiles for the addition of grout later; the lug type tiles will space themselves automatically about $\frac{1}{16}$-inch apart. Press the tiles into place with a slight twisting motion, but don't force adhesive up between the tiles. After a row of tiles has been set up, use a solid piece of wood to exert pressure on the face of the tiles to level adjoining tiles.

The floating type of adhesive (which can be used after the starting course of tile has been set with the buttering adhesive) is spread on the wall surface with the slotted trowel (Fig. 1). Cover a large wall area with the floating type before starting to tile, since it doesn't set up for an hour.

If possible, start on the wall having the least number of breaks for pipes or accessories, and work clockwise around the room. At inside wall corners, set tiles according to Fig. 15. As you near the top limit of the wall area to be tiled, lay out a line $\frac{1}{8}$-inch below the top edge of the last wall tile or cap. This line will be the top limit for the adhesive, and will prevent spreading hard-to-remove adhesive on the untiled portion.

Ceramic Tiling Your Bathroom

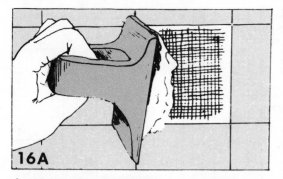

▲ *(A) Installing accessory in open space left when tiling and before grouting. Excess Keene's cement is forced around screen mesh in hole to hold accessories in place. (B) Wire basket keeps cement from falling into wall space, helps grip cement on lug. Finish flush with sides.* ▼

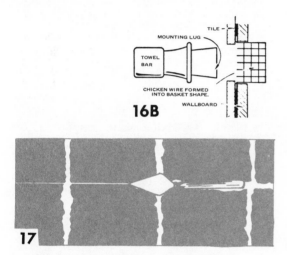

▲ *Pointing grout between joints with rounded end of seed marking stick.*

Setting bathroom accessories. After completing the wall tile work, the accessories are set in place. Cut out the holes in the wall to clear their mounting lugs. Use finishing plaster cement (sold by building supply houses) for setting them, as it sets rapidly and is white in color. Fill the space in back of the wall cutouts with chicken or reinforcing mesh wire (formed into a cup shape) to keep the cement from falling off the accessory's mounting lug (Figs. 16A and B). Mix the cement with clean water to heavy cream consistency. Apply an ex-

cess amount of cement on the mounting lug and force it into the wall opening. Remove all excess cement on the accessory and adjoining tiles before it sets hard.

You may need to prop some heavy accessories with a wooden stick, from the opposite wall, until the cement has a chance to set. This cement becomes the grouting means around the accessories and should be finished flush with their sides.

Caulking. Some joints (such as those between the wall tile and the tub, medicine cabinet to wall tile, etc.) where there might be movement between the fixture and the wall, should be sealed with caulking compound to keep water out and the joint free from cracking, which would happen if conventional grout were used. Use the same compound wherever pipes emerge through cutouts in the tile, together with pipe rings or caps.

Grouting should not be done until at least one day after completing the tiling job. Clean up all joints of any adhesive that may have been forced up, and remove the toothpicks. Use a sharp knife or a razor blade.

For grout material use tile grout, made especially for this purpose. Use non-shrinking tile grout, mixed with clean water to a light cream consistency. Just before the grout is prepared, soak the tile joints with water to prevent the absorption of the water in the grout. Saturate a cellulose sponge or cloth with water and go over wall tile joints repeatedly. Then spread the grout mixture over the tiles with a whitewash brush. After going over the walls once, go back to the starting wall and brush it on again to fill the joints. After the grout has set a few minutes, remove excess grout with a small squeegee. Then, using a wooden stick (Fig. 17) finish the joints flush with the glazed surface of the tile. Don't forget to grout the top edge of the bull nose cap and the corners as well. Sponge off walls after grout has set.

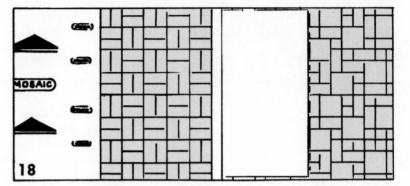

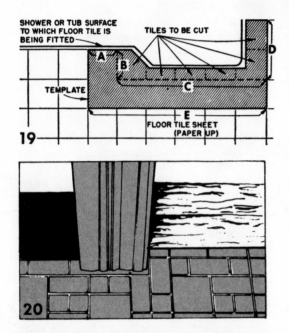

▲ *Fig. 18., Typical floor tile patterns come in sheets like this, the papered side being the top side of the tile. Fig. 19. When fitting floor tile around irregular surfaces., first cut Kraft paper holding tiles together along lines A, B, C, and D. Then make cardboard template (shaded area) to fit curvature with its lower edge even with tile division line B. Lay template even with line E, and lay tiles to be cut under template, paper up. Finally mark tiles, cut them, and attach them back to tile sheet with Scotch tape.* ◀

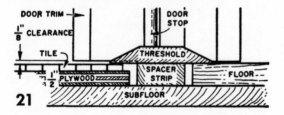

▲ *How floor tiles fit around and under door opening. Note how the tile sheet ends.* ▼

eral sheets of the floor tile pattern you select and try laying them lengthwise or crosswise on the floor area, to determine which arrangement gives you the least number of joints between the sheets. If your walls are square, then cutting the sheets to size should be easy.

Lay as many of the full tile sheets as you can around the floor area, with the paper side up. Then, starting in one corner measure the distance remaining from the edge of the sheet to the walls. Lay off this distance on top of the paper on a full floor tile sheet. Cut this sheet along the paper between the tiles nearest to the layout line. If the layout line comes part way on some of the tiles, cut the paper at the nearest full tile space and attach the tiles that will have to be cut, temporarily at their place on the sheet, with Scotch tape. They can be swung back on the sheet to get them out of the way. Repeat this procedure with all of the partial sheets around the room. Then cut the tiles that have to be cut as you did the wall tile, and attach back to the sheets.

Setting floor tile. Floor tile is sold in sheets (Fig. 18). After selecting the pattern you want and determining the size of the sheet it comes in, you can calculate how many sheets you will need. Take sev-

You can leave a space of about ⅛-inch from the edge of the last floor tile to the wall tile.

If the closet bowl is to be left undisturbed then cut the tile out to fit around it. Otherwise, trim the tile to the closet flange after the bowl has been temporarily removed. In either case, make your cardboard template first.

Where the floor tile fits against an irregular edge (such as a tub or a shower) first make a cardboard template and from it mark up the tile sheet (Fig. 19). Figure 20 shows you how to fit tile around the door trim. Cut off the door trim so that its end is about ⅛-inch above the top of the floor tile. When the tile is being set, slip the edge of the tile sheet which fits under the door trim under first. Note, in Fig. 21, how the tile sheet ends, and a space is left before the floor in the hall starts. Over this space an oak threshold is placed, supported by a spacer strip, the threshold covering the ends of the tile and the hall flooring, and extending from one side of the door frame to the other.

Remember to mark the tile sheets so you'll know where they are to fit on the floor. Finish trimming all sheets before spreading adhesive on the floor.

After priming the floor and allowing the primer to set up hard, spread the floor type of adhesive over the floor area, using the saw tooth trowel previously described, leaving no bare spots, and working yourself toward the door. Don't forget to put adhesive on the floor under the door trim. After the adhesive has set up for 15 minutes, put down small boards to stand on while you put down the tile sheets. Apply the tile sheets within 30 minutes after spreading the adhesive, using a short sliding motion, and aligning the sheets carefully with each other. Don't slide too far, or the adhesive will be forced up between the tiles, making it difficult to grout properly.

Within a half hour after the sheets have been set, remove the heavy kraft paper on top of the tile sheets by wetting it with a sponge until the glue softens enough for you to peel the paper off. Do any adjusting of the individual tiles now and use a straight edge, if necessary, to level the top surface of the tile. Place boards on the tile while working, so you won't stand or kneel directly on them, forcing individual tiles lower than the rest into the adhesive.

Grouting floor tile. Grout floor tile as you did the wall tile. The grout mixture should fill spaces between individual tiles completely. After allowing it to set a while, go over the joints with the wooden stick to get the grout slightly below the surface of the tile.

In addition, you will need to "cure" the floor grout, after cleaning it off, by covering the finished floor with damp burlap bags for three days. Cover the burlap with building paper to prevent the evaporation of water.   N.R.

◄ *A simpler alternative method of cutting tile calls for nothing more than a glass cutter, a rule and a finishing nail, but it is not recommended for big jobs. It works this way. Score the tile with the glass cutter. Place the tile on the floor over the finishing nail, so the nail is under the score. Press down each side of the tile and it will snap along the scored line.*

Plastic Bathroom Walls

Do-it-yourself kits for bathroom walls of Formica, simulated marble and fiberglass are simple to install

Y OU CAN BEAUTIFY and wet-proof your bathroom easily with any of several plastic wall coverings. These materials are durable, impervious to moisture and simple to clean, and installation is not difficult so you can cut expenses by doing the work yourself.

Formica panel system. This wall paneling is ideal for remodeling home wet areas (bathroom, laundry, kitchen) because it eliminates all the deficiencies that made older types of plastic wall coverings less than perfect. Special two-part, lock-together moldings waterproof

◄ *Plastic wall surfacing adds beauty and utility to this bathroom. The material used here is Formica.*

▼ *Begin installation of Formica Panel System 202 by measuring and laying out the base molding for inside and outside corners. Base molding is either nailed through wall to studs or attached to surface with Formica 120 Adhesive Activator where there are no studs or where moldings are being installed over tile.*

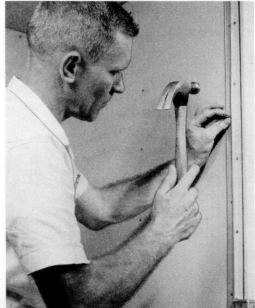

▲ When panel section has been cut to fit, give it a dry fit on the wall to make sure its size is correct. Paper templates, like the one on the wall at left, increase accuracy and reduce fitting time.

▼ After the fit of the panels has been checked, apply a liberal coating of 120 Activator to the perimeter of the wall area to be covered with the panel. Use a mohair paint roller, never a brush. Remove protective film from back of panel and apply the activator to the yellow adhesive coating.

▲ Give the activated surface time to get sticky, then test it by pressing your thumb on the surface. If you can lift the whole end of a panel in this manner, wait five minutes and apply panel to wall.

▶ Once the panels are in place, install the molding by driving the serrated tongue into the gripper groove of the base molding that was installed at the beginning of the job.

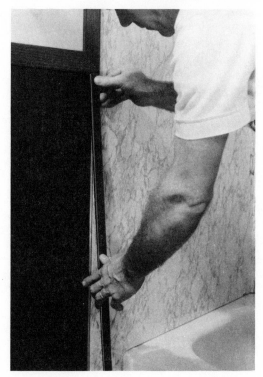

▲ *After you are certain that the walls and tub top are clean, trial fit the Corian tub enclosure kit in place. Remove it, then measure plumbing positions and mark the appropriate panel.*

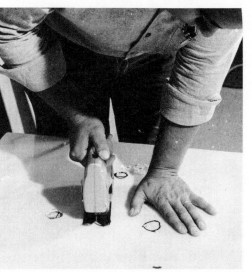

▲ *Plumbing openings are drilled. Enlarge them with a saber saw just enough to accommodate pipe, but keep them small enough so the fixtures will conceal the holes.*

and conceal all unsightly seams and keep the outer edges of the panels from popping loose. Equally important, the panels are backed with polystyrene foam so that minor irregularities on the original wall cannot possibly weaken the cement bond between wall and panel.

Identified as *Panel System 202,* this product from Formica Corp. eliminates all the headaches associated with loose, dirty grout as well as with chipping, cracking and crumbling. It wipes clean with a damp cloth, and all of the more than twenty patterns and woodgrains will keep their beauty for the life of the installation, according to the manufacturer. In the bathroom you can finish the walls using one pattern, and apply a harmonizing pattern or woodgrain on doors, trim and cabinets to achieve a sparklingly modern look.

You'll need only the basic carpenter's hand tools found in most homes, plus such other items as a couple of short nap mohair paint rollers and a rubber "J" roller. Hole cutting is easier if you also have a saber

saw (fine tooth blade), and a smarter fitting of molding miters will result if you can borrow a hacksaw miter box with clamps and saw.

Although the foam backing can cope with minor irregularities in the base surface, it cannot deal with extreme buckling of the base wall. To obtain a first-rate job, start with a smooth, clean and dry base. Then follow the detailed step-by-step instructions you can obtain from your local supplier of *System 202* paneling (we show only the principal steps in this article).

The panels are available in the following sizes: 3x8, 4x8, 5x6, 5x8 and 5x10 feet. The aluminum moldings (in 6, 8, and 10-foot lengths) are in two pieces that snap together. The female section is applied to the wall before the panel. The male section, which has a decorated laminated outer plastic surface, is snapped in place after the panel is installed.

DuPont Corian. One of the newer home improvement materials to come out of chemical research laboratories is a metha-

⋏ Use caulking gun to apply a horizontal strip of mastic at top and bottom of area on wall to be covered by the panel. Then apply vertical beads six to eight inches apart.

⋏ Install an end panel first. When you are sure it is straight, press it firmly into the mastic. Then, peel off the panel's protective coating carefully.

crylate plastic that feels and looks for all the world like a fine grade of marble. Called *Corian* by maker DuPont, the material offers several advantages over natural stone: it is easier to shape and fabricate, less expensive to buy, and it can be cut and drilled using ordinary shop tools.

The delicately-veined synthetic stone comes in several shades. Since the marble-like veins run throughout the entire thickness of the material, they cannot be worn or scrubbed off. *Corian* can be cleaned using ordinary soap or detergent and water; an occasional stubborn stain can be removed with household cleanser.

When used in the bathroom, very little cutting or drilling of the material is required other than boring holes to take wall-mounted water taps and shower heads, and cutting border trim strips to proper lengths. These modifications can be handled easily by a professional craftsman, or by anyone handy with ordinary shop tools.

A new *Corian* bathtub enclosure kit offers an easy way to remodel your tub en-

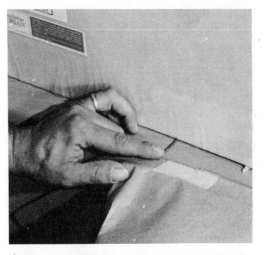

⋏ Six penny finishing nails are inserted under the panel edge to form a space for caulking at the end of the job.

closure to give it that rich, marblelike look you associate with custom-built bathrooms. Such an enclosure would look especially elegant if you also use a vanity top and bowl made of the same material.

▲ *The second panel to be installed in the Corian kit is the opposite end panel. Then install backwall side sheets, using mastic and nail shims each time.*

▲ *Hardboard fill-in sheet goes between the two backwall side panels. Again use mastic and shims. Apply mastic to exposed surface of the hardboard.*

▲ *Before installing the center panel over the hardboard, run a bead of caulking material down the edge of each Corian panel adjacent to the hardboard.*

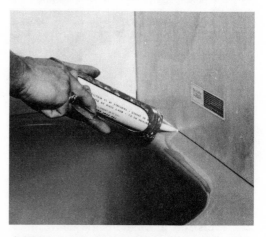

▲ *Remove nail shims and caulk space between paneling and tub top, the joints where the center panel meets the backwall side panels and the outside edges of the end panels.*

The basic kit consists of five panels, each ¼-inch thick and 57 inches high. Two side panels, measuring 29⁵⁄₁₆-inches in width, cover the side walls of almost any bathtub enclosure. Two back corner panels, each 15¼-inches wide, are fitted to the left and right rear corners of the tub area, and the space between them is covered with still another panel that is 30½-inches wide. The center panel overlaps the end panels,

thus a ¼-inch thick tempered hardboard filler (supplied with the kit) must be used behind it. An optional installation accessory kit contains two tubes of neoprene-base panel adhesive and a tube of caulking compound for finishing the joints between panels. The panels can be cemented directly to plaster, gypsum board or to ceramic tile. There's also a trim kit consisting of four strips of *Corian* material measuring

◄ *Swan Tubwal bath enclosure can be installed in about an hour, if no extra work on the walls is required.*

▼ *The system comprises three sections, two end pieces, including corners, and a center section with molded-in soap dish. All three sections are made of fiberglass.*

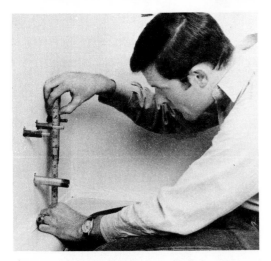

▲ *First installation step is find location of plumbing holes and mark them on the appropriate section.*

➤ *Use drill or hole saw to cut plumbing openings just large enough to accommodate pipe. Then trial fit the section.*

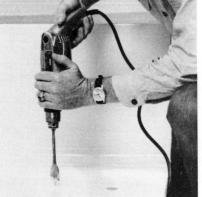

¾ x 2 x 74 inches. These strips are cut to appropriate lengths and installed as trim around the edges of the large sheets.

Don't worry about cutting the material. Although it feels and looks like honest-to-goodness marble, it can be cut and drilled using ordinary tools, according to the manufacturer.

You are unlikely to find *Corian* lavatories or tub enclosure kits in a regular lum-ber yard or other home building supply outlet. The primary outlets are kitchen and bathroom dealers specializing in the remodeling of these home areas. *Corian* should also be available at so-called "home improvement centers" that cater to the material needs of do-it-yourself homeowners.

Swan panel system. A fiberglass panel system, designed for do-it-yourself renovation of bathtub enclosures, is offered by

210

The Swan Corp. The panels are adjustable for areas measuring 63 x 30 inches or less. They can be installed over any hard and dry existing wall surface, including ceramic tile.

A center panel overlaps each of two side panels, and a unique sealing system permits adjustment to fit the paneling to most tub enclosures. The corners are rounded and seamless, hence they require no cutting,

▲ Panel is attached to wall simply by being pressed into place.

▼ Center panel goes in last. When all three sections are installed, finish the job by caulking the space where panel bottom joins the tub. Replace the plumbing fixtures.

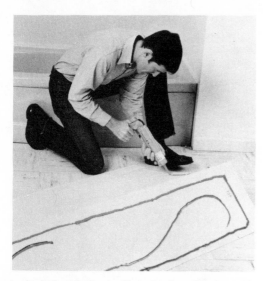

▲ Install end pieces first. Apply adhesive with a caulking gun, as shown.

▼ Remove backing—the factory-applied pressure-sensitive tape around the edge of panel.

mitering or fitting. The paneling is easily installed using a combination of pressure sensitive tape and mastic, and there are no extra moldings to apply to the edges. If necessary, the panels can be cut easily to fit around existing windows. The units all have molded-in soapdishes, and you have a choice of color.

See also: WALL COVERINGS.

▲ *Batteries come in many shapes, sizes, capacities, and construction features. This one has a prismatic cell cap for a visual indication of whether or not water is needed.*

Guarding Your Car's Battery

Get more life and reliability out of your battery with a few simple maintenance procedures

P ITY THE POOR car battery. At best it is ignored by its owner; at worst it is abused brutally. And yet it takes its punishment stoically, with hardly a complaint.

Toward the very end of its life, the battery tries to warn its owner in a tactful way —perhaps by sulfating its posts or by faltering momentarily when cranking the engine. At last, after perhaps two years of thankless toil, it abruptly expires. Has its owner learned his lesson? Hardly. He simply buys a new battery to abuse.

Fortunately, the battery manufacturers have given up on the average motorist and are busily developing permanently sealed batteries that will hold up. In fact, your car may have a sealed battery, but more likely it does not.

If it doesn't, you should give the battery some service. It requires very little—just keep it reasonably clean, satisfy its modest thirst, check its strength occasionally and extend a few other common sense courtesies.

To better understand a battery's needs, you first must understand what it is and how it works. To begin with, a battery doesn't manufacture electrical energy; it simply stores it, and then delivers it on demand. Energy is fed into a battery in the form of direct-current electricity, stored in the form of chemical energy, and released again as direct-current electricity. When a battery is accepting current, it is "charging"; delivering current, it is "discharging."

A battery consists of several cells, each containing two groups of plates made of unlike metals. These plates are immersed in electrolyte, a chemical solution that reacts with them chemically. In the lead-acid automotive battery, the positive plate is made up of lead peroxide; the negative plate is made up of a different form of lead oxide called sponge lead. Though both of these materials basically are lead, they react like unlike metals. When they are submerged in the electrolyte—a solution of sulfuric acid and water—a voltage is set up and electrical current flows when the circuit is completed. During discharge, the sulfuric acid combines with the active materials in the positive and negative plates and gradually changes both to lead sulfate. If this change is allowed to go on to completion, the battery no longer has two dissimilar metals, and electrical current no longer flows. The battery is then completely discharged.

A discharged battery must be recharged before it can deliver electricity again. This is done by applying direct current from an external source (the car generator or alternator, or a plug-in battery charger) to the battery terminals. From the terminals the current passes through the battery, in the opposite direction to the current flow when the battery is discharging. This restores the sulfated plates to their original forms—the positive plates to lead peroxide, the negative plates to sponge lead—while the sulfuric acid returns to the electrolyte. With two unlike metals in an acid solution, the battery is ready to deliver electricity again.

This cycle can't repeat itself indefinitely. Sometimes, as the plates turn to lead sulfate, large, hard crystals form that can't be broken down by recharging. Also, some of the plate material occasionally flakes off the plates and sinks to the bottom of the

battery. If enough of this material accumulates, it can short-circuit a cell. Also, a battery can suffer internal damage from excessively high temperatures, rough treatment, and other causes.

Measuring a battery's strength. Acid is heavier than water. Thus, when all the acid returns to the electrolyte during recharging, the electrolyte becomes heavier. This change can be measured in terms of specific gravity—the weight of the electrolyte as compared with an equal volume of water. From this it follows that the specific gravity of the electrolyte is an excellent indication of the state of charge of a battery.

Here is where the hydrometer comes in. A simple, inexpensive instrument, it is a wise investment for any motorist. It consists of a calibrated float in a syringe-like glass or transparent plastic tube, into which a sample of the electrolyte in each battery cell can be drawn with a rubber suction ball. When specific gravity is high, the float rises higher in the electrolyte than when specific gravity is low.

At 80° F. the specific gravity of the electrolyte in a fully-charged battery should be 1.260 or higher; discharged, 1.160 or lower. (Deduct .004 from these figures for each 10° that the battery exceeds 80°; add .004 for each 10° below 80°.) All cells should test within .050 of each other. A greater variation indicates the battery must be replaced.

A discharged battery will freeze more easily in winter. For example, a battery with a hydrometer reading of 1.140 will freeze at 8° F., while a battery with a 1.280 reading will freeze at *minus* 92°. A hydrometer check every few weeks can help extend battery life and prevent annoying failures.

A small charger is helpful, especially in winter or whenever heavy demands are made on the battery.

Such home chargers, however, are not too effective for recharging a badly run-

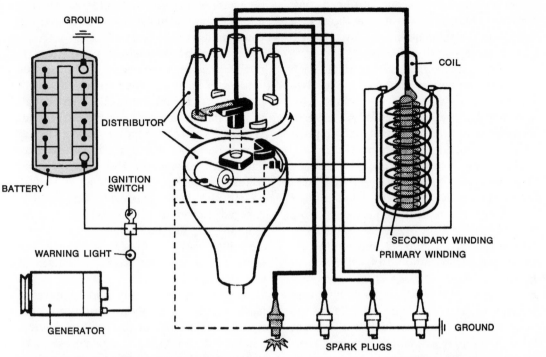

GROUND

COIL

DISTRIBUTOR

IGNITION SWITCH

BATTERY

WARNING LIGHT

SECONDARY WINDING
PRIMARY WINDING

GENERATOR

GROUND

SPARK PLUGS

⚠ *Heart of the ignition system is the battery, which supplies the spark that ignites the fuel mixture in the cylinders. While the engine is running, the generator or alternator generates electrical power.*

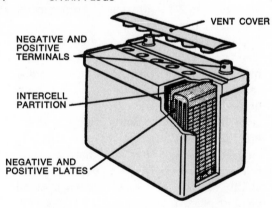

VENT COVER

NEGATIVE AND POSITIVE TERMINALS

INTERCELL PARTITION

NEGATIVE AND POSITIVE PLATES

➤ *Basic battery components are shown here. Multiply the number of cells by two to determine voltage. The capacity depends on the size and number of the plates.*

down battery. Here a larger commercial charger, as found in service stations, is needed. If possible, have the battery slow-charged; this may take from 12 to 24 hours. In cases of urgency, a fast charge (30 to 90 minutes) may be applied to get the battery up to about 70 or 80 percent of capacity. There is no risk of damage provided the battery is healthy and the current is reduced progressively. Careful supervision is necessary to make sure the battery temperature doesn't exceed 125° F. Excessive temperatures can buckle and ruin the plates.

Before placing the battery back in service, check the voltage regulator and generator or alternator output against the manufacturer's specs: too low an output causes discharging, while too high an output raises the battery temperature and increases chemical activity; either way the battery can suffer permanent damage.

Buying a battery. If your battery is defective and must be replaced, what should you look for in a new one? The first consideration, obviously, is outside dimensions. The new battery must fit the holder; a loose, improperly-mounted battery will quickly bounce itself to death.

Secondly, the voltage must be right. Each cell in a car battery puts out about two volts; thus a six-volt battery has three cells, a 12-volt battery has six cells. All modern domestic cars and practically all imports have 12-volt electrical systems.

For many years, batteries have been rated according to their ability, when fully charged, to deliver a specified quantity of electricity over a definite period of time (usually 20 hours). Basically, capacity is determined by the number and size of the plates and by the amount of sulfuric acid in the electrolyte. It is expressed in ampere-hours, a unit of measure obtained by multiplying the current flow in amperes by the time in hours during which the current flows. For example, a battery delivering five amperes for 20 hours has a 100-ampere-hour capacity.

Battery capacity also is rated in watts. The "Peak Watts Rating" is a measurement of starting power, with 3,000 the normally required Peak Watts Rating for the battery needed by the average car.

In fact, the Peak Watts Rating was the first successful attempt to supplant the amp-hour rating. After all, what you want is a measurement of starting power, not the ability of the battery to deliver a small amount of current over a 20-hour period. The amp-hour rating might be a convenient way of telling if your battery will have any juice left if you leave the parking lights on overnight, but that is about all.

There actually is a rating that gives you an indication of starting power. Called the "Five-Second Voltage," it indicates the number of volts the battery can maintain at zero degrees after a starting drain of 150 amps.

A good battery would have a rating of 9.4 to 10.2 volts. Of course, starting am-perage draw is greater than 150 (more like 350-500 amps), but at least this rating tells you something.

Under a newer system, the battery is rated in amperes discharged in 30 seconds without voltage dropping to less than 1.2 per cell (7.2 for the battery)—high enough to start the car until perhaps the last second. With this system, a good battery would have a rating in excess of 375, a premium battery in excess of 450. To calculate reserve capacity, another newer rating counts the number of minutes a fully-charged battery at 80° F. will deliver 25 amps—indicating how long you can drive a car with a defective generator and still use important accessories, such as windshield wipers, lights, etc.

A replacement battery should have at least as great a capacity as the original one. If your engine isn't in the best mechanical condition and requires lots of cranking, or if you've added electrical accessories since buying the car, splurge for a greater capacity (heavy-duty) battery. An under-powered, bargain-basement battery is no bargain; it will give poor service right from the start, and will fail sooner.

Mounting the battery. Secure the battery hold-down straps snugly, but not so tightly as to crack the battery case. Examine the battery cables, and replace them if they are suspect. Remove corrosion from terminals by dipping them in a solution of sodium bicarbonate and water and then flushing with clean water. If necessary, wire brush the terminals and battery posts lightly for good electrical contact. If the terminals fit the posts too loosely, wind copper wire tightly around the posts. Attach the ground cable last to avoid short circuits. (When removing the battery, reverse this procedure and loosen the ground cable first.)

Once the terminals are on clean and tight, lightly coat them and the top of the battery post with petroleum jelly. Do not apply this coating to the sides of the battery

➤ *If a battery is questionable, it should be checked with a battery-starter tester. One shown is an inexpensive type that a weekend mechanic might consider.*

posts before the terminals are attached, or you will impede current flow.

On General Motors cars with the sealed side terminals, the only service necessary is to occasionally check the cable terminal for corrosion and wire brush if necessary, making certain the terminal is tight. Don't grease anything.

Once the battery is installed, make sure connections are made properly. Turning on the headlights should show a discharge reading on your ammeter (if you're lucky enough to have one in your car) or, with ignition key on and the engine not running, should cause your generator warning light to glow. If the ammeter shows charge or the warning light doesn't glow, turn the battery around and switch the connections. Finally, smear the terminals and posts with petroleum jelly to reduce corrosion.

Keeping your battery healthy. Check the electrolyte level in each cell at least twice a month (more often during hot weather or fast, long-distance driving). As electricity passes through the cells, some of the water in the electrolyte is converted into hydrogen and oxygen gases and escapes through the vent holes in the battery caps. Normally a battery uses only a slight amount of water every few weeks. An excessive thirst indicates overcharging; check the electrical system.

Experts disagree on whether ordinary tap water may be added to a battery. Some say naturally soft, clear tap water is acceptable, but most recommend using distilled water (sold in auto accessory stores), rain water gathered in non-metallic containers, or clean melted snow. Rather than letting a service station attendant fill your battery, you'd be wise to carry your own plastic bottle of distilled water in the trunk. Never add acid to a battery; this subjects the plates to higher current densities, causing faster deterioration.

Check electrolyte level with a flashlight if necessary, but never with a match or other open flame; gases produced by batteries are highly explosive. Most batteries have markers to show proper electrolyte level. If yours doesn't, fill each cell no more than $3/8$-inch above the plates. When the electrolyte level drops below the tops of the plates, the concentration of acid increases dangerously. Overfilling also is harmful. As battery temperatures rise, the electrolyte expands until it overflows through the vents. It then can form a bridge on top of the battery across which current can flow, draining the battery. Or it may damage the battery holder, body panels, and engine.

Special battery fillers are available that stop water flow automatically when proper electrolyte level has been reached. In a pinch, use your hydrometer to fill the battery. Pouring in water from a cup or bottle is unwise; the flow is hard to control.

In cold weather, add water only if you plan to run the car immediately afterward. Otherwise the water may freeze and crack the battery case. Also, do not take hydrometer reading immediately after adding water.

Those "miraculous" additives. Notwithstanding the fantastic claims made by manufacturers of various battery additives, none of these products has been proved effective in rejuvenating or extending the life of a healthy battery; more likely, additives will ruin your battery and void the warranty.

If the electrolyte level in one cell drops faster than in the others, suspect a leak. Small cracks in the battery case can be sealed with pitch or commercial sealer applied with a soldering gun. A large crack will necessitate replacement of the battery. Only when refilling a repaired cell should you use an acid solution. Check with a hydrometer to make sure you get the right concentration.

Besides checking electrolyte level, and state of charge and cleaning away corrosion, what else can you do to add years to the life of your battery? For one thing, you can keep your engine well-tuned and your starter motor in top condition to reduce current drain during starting. Also, remember the following driving hints:

Before starting the engine, shut off headlights and other electrical equipment. If you have a manual transmission, shift into neutral and hold the clutch disengaged. Cold, viscous transmission oil puts a considerable drag on transmission gears; but with the clutch (and transmission) disengaged, the starter motor has to crank just the engine.

On cold days, keep the battery warm, if possible. A fully charged battery at 0° F.

loses 60 percent of the cranking power it has at 80°; and an engine at 0° requires two and a half times as much starting power as at 80°. That's why a weak battery may get you through the summer, but will fail during the first cold snap. Inexpensive battery warmers that plug into a household outlet are available.

In slow-moving, stop-and-go traffic, especially at night, when headlights are in use, avoid using other electrical accessories if possible. When traffic comes to a stop for a few minutes, switch down from headlights to parking lights (but don't forget to switch back when you start moving).

Jumper cables are good to have in your trunk—just in case. If you should have to use them, be sure you wire the posts of the two batteries from positive to positive and negative to negative; otherwise the wiring and other components may be damaged. The posts of most batteries are marked.

According to battery manufacturers, the average life of a car battery is 26 months. And yet some savvy motorists have squeezed five years' service from their batteries—evidence that a little tender loving care pays big benefits.   P. W.

See also: ALTERNATOR, AUTO; DC GENERATOR, AUTO; ELECTRICAL, AUTO; IGNITION SYSTEM, AUTO.

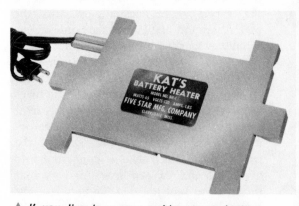

▲ *If you live in a very cold area, a battery heater can make winter starting easier. The battery heater is placed in the bottom of the battery case, the battery sits on it, and the heater is plugged into a household outlet.*

Buying a Battery for Your Boat

**A penny saved on this item
could mean many dollars lost
later on. Base your choice on
quality and cost per month**

A BATTERY is a utility item, hidden under the hatch or in some other inaccessible place, out of sight and out of mind so long as the engine starts and the electrical system works. To most boatmen the battery is the algebraic "X," the unknown quantity, an obscure black box that may suddenly conk out—always at the most embarrassing time.

In buying a battery, the top grade is usually the most economical in the long run. There is no skimping on material, and being a bit oversize it stores more energy to start the engine under conditions that cause low-grade batteries to fail. The savings in recharges and other service more than offset the additional cost of the quality battery.

When you buy a battery you will find there is an *initial* cost and an *actual* cost. The initial cost is the price you pay for the battery off the dealer's shelf. The actual cost involves what you pay initially, plus money paid for upkeep, measured against length of service received.

For example, a battery costing $30 and lasting three years without need of recharging or other service costs about 84¢ a month. A gyp battery for $10 that lasts a year and needs two recharges during that time costs you about $1.08 a month. In the latter case the cost and inconvenience of having the battery fail at sea are not included.

Since there are great differences between batteries, it's well worthwhile to select a battery with a well-known trade name rather than just any battery offered you. You will save money by buying a battery that has earned a name and a reputation in the battery field.

One mistake commonly made by the boatman in buying a battery is to buy one too small to do the job. In a car, lights, radio, and other accessories are used while the engine is running, and the generator supplies the necessary current. But in a boat, most of the accessories are used at anchor with the engine not running, and the battery supplies the power.

The electrical size of the battery is expressed in terms of volts and ampere-hour capacity, such as 6 volt, 100 AH, 12 volt, 50 AH, etc. The ampere-hour capacity is based on a 20-hour discharge rate and is an indication of the battery's ability to deliver power continuously over a 20-hour period. It is the measure of the amount of working material put into the battery; that is, the number and size of the plates. A 100-AH battery will deliver 5 amps continuously for 20 hours, 4 amps for a bit longer than 25 hours, or 2 amps for considerably longer than 50 hours. But it will not deliver 50 amperes for two hours or 100 amperes for one hour. No boat should have a battery smaller than 100 AH, and preferably double that, in two batteries connected in parallel or in a dual-battery automatic system.

Sometimes the electrical size of a battery is expressed in terms of the number of plates in a cell or the total number of plates in the battery. But since there is no standard for the size of the plates, such a rating has little value. Some gyp batteries have plates only half as long as the plates of a quality battery.

Most batteries are guaranteed for 90 days against defective workmanship and

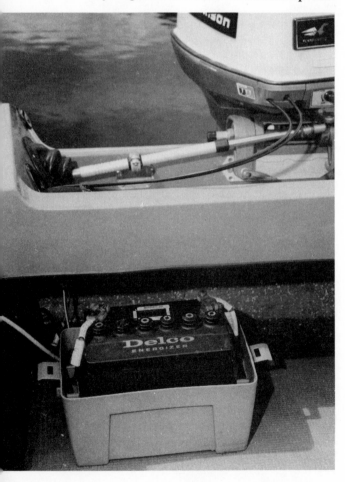

material and for a period of months of service. Such guarantees are of the pro-rata type, which means that when a battery fails to give its guaranteed service the owner is entitled to buy a replacement battery at a reduced price, based on the service received. For example, a battery costing $30, guaranteed for three years, fails at 18 months. The owner would be entitled to a new battery for $15. Note that the guarantee does not specify how well the battery will perform, nor does it protect the owner against the cost of recharging or other service. On such a basis a gyp battery, even though guaranteed for long service, can be costly. Better stick with the better-known brands.

Fundamentally, the buyer should be concerned with these things:

Will the battery operate the boat's electrical system satisfactorily? If it will not, frequent recharges will be necessary and you can be sure it will fail you at the time you need it most.

Will the battery serve dependably for a long time? If it won't you'll be faced with an early replacement, making the cost on a per month basis prohibitive.

Does the manufacturer provide adequate service? When trouble occurs, the guarantee is not much good unless the manufacturer can provide dealer service at the point where you need assistance. A battery with a guarantee backed by a nationwide dealer-service organization is highly desirable.

In batteries, as in almost everything else, you get about what you pay for. A battery offered at an unusually low price is not necessarily a bargain. It may well be a battery made to sell at that price, or even lower. The difference between a medium and a low-price battery may be only in capacity, the quality level of both being about the same. On the other hand, the low-price battery may be low in both capacity and quality.   **L. H.**

↟ *Some of the batteries that were tested for this article.*

Getting the Most Out of Small Batteries

How, what and why of buying power for flashlights, radios and toys

CONSUMERS in the USA spend five times more money on flashlight and transistor batteries every year than on vitamin pills—over $310 million for batteries and $68 million for vitamins. The federal government tests the vitamins and has established strict labeling requirements for them. Not so with batteries!

The label on many of those batteries bought at your favorite neighborhood store have their date of manufacture stamped on them—but it's concealed and coded so you'll never know how old the batteries are. While the dimensions of batteries are carefully regulated by government and industry agreements, the contents are not.

To find out once and for all how various kinds of batteries do hold up under typical use—not how well they hold up according to glossy advertising claims—statistical tests were set up to run piles of batteries to death. Flashlights aimed at commercially available photocells tested lighting applications of "D" sized batteries. Toys, which involve small DC motors instead of light bulbs, place an entirely different demand on batteries. A small battery powered electric train was set up on a circular track running past a lap counter to test the stamina of every battery shoved into the engineer's seat. Those noisy little transistor radios place a very low drain on very small power cells (about .020 amps for a radio compared with .5 amps for some common flashlights). Sound switches on microphones controlled the timers which measured the life span of "AA" sized batteries used in transistor radios.

Almost without exception, the test results can be summed up in a single, surprising conclusion. For the sake of both economy and overall performance, the cheapest batteries you can buy may very well be your wisest choice!

Results from the toy train test are recorded below in number of *laps per penny of battery cost* for continuous, one-shot battery life. (Kids very often play with their toys continuously until the batteries wear out. Next day, it's "next set of batteries, Pop.")

Made in USA		*Imported*
STANDARD	LONG LIFE	STANDARD
5.59	13.64	list price 15.30
6.15	15.00	10% disc.
6.71	16.37	20% disc.
8.38	20.46	33% disc.

If you buy made-in-USA batteries at their list price (generally printed on the cell itself), the imports come out to be your best buy according to the test train.

BATTERY RECOMMENDATIONS

Plan ahead when selecting any appliance that will need batteries. If the item is going to receive heavy or frequent use, the larger battery sizes (for the same power output) are doubly preferred. They have a more stable shelf life and all batteries perform relatively longer when drained at levels well below the maximum they can handle. An "AA" cell and a "D" cell both can handle the .3 and .5 amp drain of a flashlight, but the "D" cell would more than pay for itself with longer life because its recommended load rating is six times that of a comparable "AA" cell.

Novelty items and gadgets used only infrequently should accommodate the smallest, cheapest variety of battery available.

Purpose	Intermittent Use	Frequent Use
TRANSISTOR RADIOS:	Cheapest available, changed often to avoid leaking which will damage the radio.	(1) Standard carbon-zinc cells designed for transistor applications. (2) Rechargeable nickel-cadmium (best) or rechargeable alkaline cells.
FLASHLIGHTS:	Cheapest available, changed often.	(1) Still, the cheapest available, or (2) Rechargeable nickel-cadmium or alkaline cells. They are quite expensive initially although economical over the long run.
TOYS:	Cheapest available, changed often.	Rechargeables.
ELECTRONIC FLASH UNITS, TAPE RECORDERS:	Cheapest available, changing often.	Alkaline cells or rechargeables.
CLOCKS, WRIST WATCHES, HEARING AIDS:	Battery designed and guaranteed for the specific application. (Watch and hearing aid batteries are not always interchangeable.)	

The alkaline or manganese (they're essentially the same except for the advertising pitch) "long life" cells proved to last from two to four times longer than imported standard batteries. And the long life cells out-lived standard made-in-USA cells by three to eight times. But the cost per lap for alkaline batteries was higher if you bought them at list price. Even a 10 percent discount is not enough to beat the economy of imports. If the long life USA batteries can be bought at 15 percent or more off list price, then they become cheaper within the limitations of their test—in continuous, heavy duty use.

Discounts were not figured into the price comparisons for imported batteries. Some of them have "list prices" marked on the case, but seldom do those prices bear much resemblance to sales reality. None of the batteries sold under the names of well-known imported electrical appliance makers were included in the battery tests, the preference going to unknown, strictly price-promoted merchandise.

All batteries tested were bought at a dozen or so different stores ranging from expensive department stores through "dime stores."

Continuous tests to exhaustion for flashlight batteries came up with statistics very comparable to exhaustive tests for use in toys. The USA long lifes held out for an average of 13 hours, the imported long life batteries averaged about 12 hours, imported standard cells burned for over six hours straight, and at the bottom, the USA standards pushed on for barely over five hours before the bulb flickered out.

However flashlights, unlike toys, are seldom used continuously around the house. Around shops frequented by mechanics, plumbers and repairmen, the use is considerably heavier than around the house. So a variety of intermittent use tests were made.

The flashlights were turned on for one hour a day. Toys were run through the test track one hour or one half hour every 24 hour day. All tests were done approximately the same time each day. And a second big surprise awaited—the expensive alkaline or manganese long life cells showed up in these tests as an absolute waste for long-term use.

Standard cells typically gave double the total amount of service in tests spread over several days compared with tests which wore them out in one fell swoop. The big brother alkaline cells provided about *half* the life span on rugged intermittent tests compared with what they could turn in during a single, long exhaustive test session. The conclusion? Unless your use of batteries puts such a heavy drain on them that they'll be exhausted in a day or two (such as in small electronic flash guns, tape recorders, etc.), the alkaline cells could very well return less service than standard cells even though the alkaline version cost several times more.

In order to watch for variations in the same brand, a disproportionate number of cells from one top USA brand were tested. The batteries were purchased at a discount electronic supply house, at a reputable radio and TV repair wholesaler (who assured the buyer that his shipment from the factory had just arrived), and at a discount hardware store of occasionally questioned reputation. The best in the bunch (from the discount electronic store) came out three times better than the worst (the hardware store's)—same brand, same price, precisely the same type of battery.

Engineers for the company that manufactured these batteries were obviously embarrassed when the test results were sprung on them during a two hour, altogether too friendly interview. They conceded at the outset that the test figures were probable, but said, "We don't expect more than a 10 percent fluctuation in results as the batteries leave our factory. The three-fold

▲ *Testing batteries in a toy train. Lap counter showed how far each battery went before giving out and costs were compared in terms of laps per penny of battery cost.*

variation must come from some variable other than our manufacturing." The battery engineers settled upon shelf life and storage conditions as the culprit.

Unknown to many folks, batteries are just as susceptible to heat as film. One test showed that batteries left in the trunk of a car in a Texas parking lot reached unenviable temperature of 180 degrees! That's guaranteed to shorten the life of man, beast or battery. The "Eveready Battery Applications Engineering Data" book says, "The shelf life of a battery stored at 90° F. may be one-third that of one stored at 70° F."

Even at 70° F., the useable power retained inside of batteries is very dependent upon how long they have been sitting on a shelf before being used. Battery engineers like to quote shelf life figures for their product as one year for standard carbon-zinc cells and two years for the alkaline variety. Shelf life is defined as the length of time it takes a battery fresh from the factory to lose 10 percent of its designed power. With

a bit of coaxing, however, the engineers will concede that the life span of cells smaller than "D" cells diminishes relatively quickly.

Tests run periodically and published by the American National Standards Institute, Inc., reveal just how quickly small batteries do deteriorate. ANSI is a trade association which produces industry-wide standards for products ranging from lawn mowers to light meters. Standard batteries intended for flashlight use deteriorate over six months as follows according to ANSI:

"D" size	6.25%
"C" size	15.38%
"AA" size	18.75%
"N" size	28.57%

Much the same holds true over six months for standard carbon-zinc transistor batteries according to the ANSI publication:

9-volt (round)   6.67%
9-volt (flat)   10.71%
"AA" size   20%

For the much higher-priced alkaline cells intended for transistor use, deterioration over six months is reported by ANSI to be:

"D" size   8.70%
"AA" size   13.3%

The effects of aging for six months seem to be even more pronounced when the alkaline-manganese cells are put into high discharge, continuous use such as they receive in small electronic flashes or tape recorders:

"D" size   8.75–11.1%
"AA" size   20–23.5%

The sizes of batteries which are so popular in transistor radios and similar gadgets deteriorate so quickly that if the box of cells has been sitting on a *cool* counter for six months before some hapless consumer buys them, they might provide one fifth less noise than expected. If the batteries had been sitting on a *warm* counter or in a hot storeroom for six months, one half or even more than half of the expected shelf life would be gone before the consumer ever had a chance to plug in the batteries.

It would be nice if every battery manufacturer printed the birth date on their batteries where consumers could find it. Over ten years ago that was a common practice. Alternately, they could follow the example of film manufacturers who print an approximate expiration date in plain sight. The companies that do stamp a date on their product, do so surreptitiously.

Union Carbide, for example, began stamping a two- or three-letter code on the bottom of its alkaline Eveready batteries, and on the side of its carbon-zinc cells in 1969. The Eveready code identifies the plant which turned out the battery, the year

of manufacture (the last of two or three marks), and the month in which the battery was made (the first of the markings). But the code is not made available to the public and only with extreme reluctance are they given to large consumers of batteries who use them in manufacturing or selling their own battery-powered equipment.

If your Eveready battery has a stamp reading "KR", you now will know it was made in January (K) of 1970 (R). "FB" signifies February (F) of 1971 (B). "CNU" identifies a particular plant (N), the month of June (C) in the year 1972 (U).

Aside from all of the other design problems that face battery engineers who have to pack maximum power into minimum space, they also have to contend with liquids that like to ooze out of the battery case. For longest life, the maximum amount of moisture generally must be added to the chemical mixture inside the cell. The fact that "D" cells are large enough to hold proportionally more moisture than their little brothers, the "AA" and "N" size, is the principal explanation for the fact that "D" cells have a longer shelf life.

A *zinc chloride* battery was test marketed in the fall of 1972. Putting zinc chloride inside a battery is nothing new. There is some in just about every zinc-carbon cell you buy right now. The proportion can be changed and the resulting product can be promoted as something new. More than likely the price can also be new.

The technology already exists to make flashlight batteries which last considerably longer than the ones you buy across the counter, and not at a considerable price premium. Most major battery manufacturers also make a product they label "For industrial use. Not available at retail." Going by figures published in Eveready's own data book, the "AA" size industrial battery

▲ *Date codes (above) can tell you when the battery was produced, giving you some clue as to how much power it may have lost on the shelf. On this Eveready alkaline cell, the "F" stands for February and the "U" means 1972. Don't believe advertising about "leakproof" batteries. Here are four batteries from three countries: All of them leaked. A guarantee helps, but it would be nice if they didn't leak.* ◄

lasts 25 percent longer than its standard "AA" counterpart, both given the same "light-industrial flashlight test." At the "D" size, the difference is even more noticeable. The No. 1150 industrial zinc-carbon battery has a slightly smaller diameter but weighs 10 percent more than the standard Eveready No. 950 flashlight cell. Given the same "light-industrial flashlight test" by its maker, the No. 1150 lasted 1000 minutes while its counterpart, which gets sold to you and me, lasted only 680 minutes—a 32 percent dropoff! F.P.

See also: CITIZEN'S BAND RADIO; ELECTRONICS.

Servicing Your Car's Wheel Bearings

Inspect these key parts regularly to keep your steering precise and prevent failure

WHEN YOUR CAR begins to roll as if going uphill through a bucket of glue, and wanders back and forth across the highway, it's time to have a look at those hard-working bearings whose job it is to keep your ton-and-a-half car rolling effortlessly along in a straight line at maximum speeds.

These periodic inspections and adjustments are your best safeguard against bearing failure when you can least afford it. Only the front wheels need to be inspected because only they are adjustable. Rear wheel bearings are usually not disturbed unless there is some specific reason for removing them, and, once removed, they are replaced.

To inspect your front wheel bearings, first block the car so it will not roll, and then jack up a front wheel, supporting it so the wheel can be removed. Take off the wheel cover, dust cover, cotter pin, adjust-

⋏ *Quick check for front wheel bearings is to grasp wheel at top and bottom and try to rock in and out. If you can feel play, wheel bearings should be inspected.*

ing nut (be careful, it might be a left-hand thread), and flat washer. Then carefully remove the wheel, hub and bearings at one time.

Next, lift out the small bearings at the outer end of the hub and turn the wheel over to remove the rest of the bearing assembly. First pry out the oil seal and lift out the large bearing; then remove the bearing cups.

When the bearing is removed, note the color and odor of the grease. If it looks burned—almost black—or has an acrid odor, it is a dead giveaway that the bearing has been running hot. If the grease looks and smells normal, clean each part of the bearing assembly in solvent and allow to

Servicing Your Car's Wheel Bearings

◄ *Start by prying off metal dust cover.*

▼ *Pull out cotter pin. (Be sure you have a replacement; cotter pins should not be reused.)*

▲ *Remove nut lock and then unthread castellated nut.*

➤ *Pull out on wheel and outer wheel bearing will pop out as shown.*

▼ *With wheel off, turn it over and pry out grease seal to gain access to inner wheel bearing. Parts in typical assembly are as shown.*

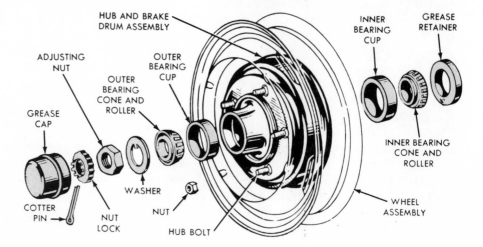

HUB AND BRAKE
DRUM ASSEMBLY

INNER
BEARING
CUP

GREASE
RETAINER

ADJUSTING
NUT

OUTER
BEARING
CUP

OUTER
BEARING
CONE AND
ROLLER

GREASE
CAP

INNER BEARING
CONE AND
ROLLER

COTTER
PIN

NUT
LOCK

WASHER

NUT

HUB BOLT

WHEEL
ASSEMBLY

Servicing Your Car's Wheel Bearings

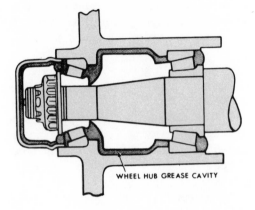

WHEEL HUB GREASE CAVITY

⬆ Wheel hub grease cavity should be cleaned with solvent and repacked. Best method is with special tool with bearings back in place. Otherwise, just coat cavity surfaces generously.

⬆ *Above: Wheel bearings should be cleaned in solvent, and allowed to air dry; then coat with wheel bearing grease as shown. Below: Torque wrench in position for adjustment of wheel bearings to manufacturer's specifications.* ⬇

dry. Do not dry the bearings by *spinning* them with a blast from an air hose as it will drive grit into the bearings.

When the bearings and cups are clean and dry, check them for signs of *brinnelling* or *spalling*. These are just two of the several ways in which wheel bearings are damaged or worn. Brinnelling is a series of indentations where the rollers have slammed into the surface of the cup (caused by severe impact, such as when a wheel goes into a rut in the road). Spalling appears as chipping or crumbling on the small ends of roller bearings (caused by excessive clearance).

Fractures will appear as fine hairline cracks across the surface of the cup or cone. These are usually a result of forcing bearings onto oversize spindles, forcing cups into warped hubs, or improperly seating the cups.

Corrosion results in pits or pock-marks and appears similar to spalling, but is located at random along the bearings and cups. It is usually an indication that moisture or road chemicals have entered the bearing through a defective seal and have contaminated the bearing grease. It is also possible for corrosion to be caused by handling a bearing when all of the oil has been washed from its surface. Ordinary perspiration is often highly corrosive, so it is good practice to handle clean bearings with a dry, lint-free cloth.

End wear is also similar to spalling, but appears on the large ends of roller bearings. It is generally caused by too-tight bearing adjustments, resulting in insufficient clearance.

Dangerous dirt. If you find any of these defects, replace the entire bearing assembly. Never replace just one or two parts as the reason for failure in one part was very likely working on the entire assembly. Also, keep the workbench, tools, lubricant, and your hands free of dirt and grime when working with bearings. Grit is the mortal enemy of free-rolling, long-lasting bearings.

When installing replacement bearings, no on-the-spot lubrication is necessary. All new bearings are prelubricated to be used just as they come from the box. Old bearings that are in good condition should be repacked with special wheel-bearing grease.

Before refitting the bearings, clean out the bearing cavity with solvent. Make sure you have a tube of wheel-bearing grease to coat the bearing cavity. Coat the cavity, then install the bearings.

Reassembly. Check the replacement races and bearings against the old parts to be sure you have the right ones. Install the races and large bearing. Then dab the seal with clean oil and start it into the hub by hand, with lip positioned. The oil will make the seal slide on the spindle easily, preventing damage during reassembly, and will also make it soft and effective as a seal immediately. Never install a seal with just a hammer or use a steel punch which could damage the casing and cause leakage. Under no circumstances ever attempt to reuse a seal. Mount the wheel carefully to avoid tearing the seal on the spindle and install the outer bearing, washer, and adjusting nut.

Adjustment. The most common forms of adjustment are illustrated in this article. In all of these, the amount of tension applied on the thrust washer by an adjusting nut is set to the manufacturer's specifications, or according to feel for lack of free play and smooth rotation of the wheel. Adjustment by feel, although reasonably accurate and practical, should be done only if a torque wrench is not available.

Note: cars with tapered roller bearings should only be set with a torque wrench if the car maker specifies a torque setting to seat the bearings.

Tapered roller bearings can be damaged by improper installation very easily.

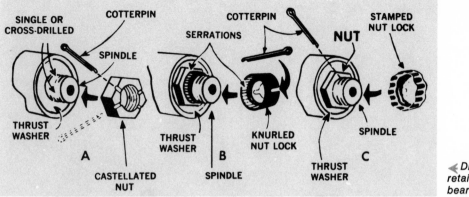

A

SINGLE OR CROSS-DRILLED — SPINDLE — COTTERPIN — THRUST WASHER — CASTELLATED NUT

B

SERRATIONS — COTTERPIN — THRUST WASHER — SPINDLE — KNURLED NUT LOCK

C

NUT — STAMPED NUT LOCK — SPINDLE — THRUST WASHER

◄*Different methods of retaining wheel and bearings are illustrated.*

To adjust a bearing by feel, first seat the bearing assembly by tightening the nut with a long wrench until you feel a definite resistance while rotating the wheel. Then loosen the nut and run it up again finger-tight. Continue tightening it with the pliers, rotating the wheel and checking for free play constantly with your other hand. Stop tightening at the point where free play has just been eliminated. Be careful not to overtighten the bearing, mistaking loose-ness, at the ball joint for free play.

Now spin the wheel, stopping at several points to check for free play, and, if necessary, tighten the nut to eliminate it. Never back off more than one slot on the nut to get to the point where free play is eliminated. If the bearing becomes too tight, back the nut off to finger-tight and start over.

Torque wrench adjustment. The exact procedure for torque wrench adjustment varies according to make of car. Here are the procedures for popular late-model cars:

Ford products: With wheel rotating, tighten adjusting nut to 17 to 25 ft./lbs. Back adjustment nut off ½ turn. Tighten adjusting nut to just one ft./lb. Install the lock nut and a new cotter pin.

Chrysler products: Tighten bearing nut to seven ft./lbs. while rotating wheel. Position nut lock so that a pair of slots lines up with the cotter pin hole. Back off the nut lock (with the nut inside it) one slot, then install the cotter pin.

Chevrolet: Tighten bearing nut to 12 ft./lbs. while rotating wheel. Back off adjusting nut one flat and attempt to insert cotter pin. If the slot and pin hole do not line up, back off the nut until they do (an additional ½ flat turn or less should do it).

Not all car makers specify a torque wrench setting, and in some cases, the nut is never to be torqued.

Cars equipped with disc brakes on the front wheels pose a special problem insofar as wheel bearing service is concerned: the caliper and disc must come off.

This means that you must remove the wheel first by unbolting it from the wheel hub.

On older cars with fixed caliper disc brakes, removing the caliper may be a chore. If possible, hang the caliper with wire from the front suspension, so you do not have to disconnect a brake line (which would force you to bleed the brakes).

Under no circumstances should you let the caliper dangle by a brake hose. This is a sure-fire way to cause a premature brake hose failure.

If you find shims under the heads of the bolts that attach the caliper to the front suspension, you must refit them as they were, for they center the caliper over the disc.

Once the caliper is off, pull the dust cap from the disc and proceed as with drum brakes.   **P.W.**

See also: BALL JOINTS; SHOCK ABSORBERS, AUTO.

How to Change Engine Bearings

This job is often easier than it sounds—it all depends on how hard it is to drop the oil pan— and doing-it-yourself can save a sizeable mechanic's bill

MOST WEEKEND MECHANICS think of engine bearings as little as possible, and then merely as the super-smooth supports for the engine's moving parts. The reasoning is that bearings are nothing for the weekend mechanic to worry about because they should last a long time, and if they don't, there is nothing he can do about it. But good maintenance practices will prolong bearing life, and if replacement is necessary for the most heavily loaded bearings—those on the crankshaft—the job often can be done by a weekend mechanic without exotic tools. Even if you have the work done by a professional, you should know what is involved and what types of crankshaft bearings are available for installation.

Let's review crankshaft properties:

Load-carrying ability. The downward pressure on the piston of the exploding gasoline mixture is transmitted by the connecting rod to the crankshaft. This pressure creates a load which must be carried by the bearings within the connecting rod and the crankshaft support caps (called the main bearing caps). The more powerful the engine, the greater the pressure developed by the exploding gasoline mixture, and the greater load.

High fatigue strength. The ability of the bearing to withstand the cumulative effect of a repeatedly applied force. In other words, the bearing can take a lot of pounding without getting "tired." (In the case of a bearing, when it gets "tired," it cracks.) The higher the fatigue strength, the longer the bearing will last under a certain load.

Slipperiness. When the engine is being cranked, and under other severe conditions, there is no oil film to provide lubrication. So the bearing surfaces must have a natural slipperiness, to avoid scoring the journals (the mirror-smooth round surfaces of the crankshaft, around which the bearings are fitted).

Corrosion resistance. As a result of combustion, corrosive agents are formed in the oil pan. The engine oil contains additives that neutralize these corrosive agents, but if the additives are used up, the bearing itself must be resistant to corrosion.

Ability to withstand high temperatures. Crankcase temperatures can exceed 200 degrees, which can affect the strength of a bearing material.

Conformability. Manufacturing tolerances prevent the bearing surface from being exactly parallel with the journal surface it supports. The ability of a bearing material to "creep" or "flow" to be reasonably parallel is called conformability.

Heat transfer. Both the oil and the bearings must transfer heat from the cylinders. The bearing must do its part of the job.

No one metal can do everything, so bearings are made of layers of different metals. The usual procedure is to use a steel backing for maximum overall strength and a top layer of babbitt, an alloy of tin and lead. Babbitt has superb natural slip-periness and conformability, making it an ideal bearing material in these respects. It also has good "embeddability," which means it can "absorb" dirt particles so they can't score journals. (With today's oil filters, embeddability isn't overly significant, but it's helpful in cases where the oil filter isn't changed at proper intervals.)

Unfortunately, babbitt has relatively low fatigue strength and load-carrying ability. So a layer of babbitt on a steel back would work only in light-duty applications. In such cases, either a lead-base or tin-base babbitt is used. The lead base has a slightly higher load-carrying ability.

Today's powerful engines use bearings with a layer of a secondary bearing material between a thin babbitt outer layer and the steel backing. This design serves two

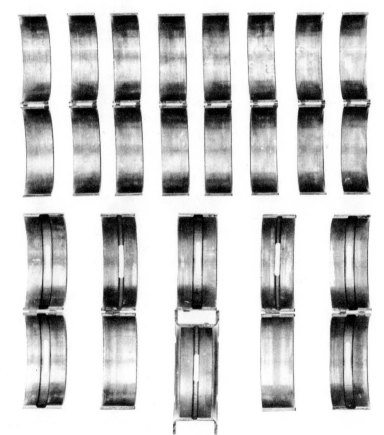

▶ *These are the engine's main and connecting rod bearings. The eight sets of connecting rod bearings and five sets of main bearings are for typical V-8.*

purposes: The thin babbitt layer (.0005 to .0015 inch) actually has a higher fatigue strength than a thick layer; that is, it is less prone to cracking. However, once the babbitt layer wears through, there has to be a reasonably suitable bearing surface. The usual choices for the second bearing layer are sintered (powdered) copper-lead, aluminum alloy, cadmium nickel and cast copper-lead. It is the second layer that essentially determines the bearing's load-carrying ability.

Cadmium nickel has better fatigue strength and load-carrying ability than babbitt, but isn't as slippery, doesn't conform as well, and has far less embeddability. It is sometimes plated with indium for greater corrosion resistance.

Aluminum alloy: a very satisfactory bearing material for medium to fairly heavy-duty use.

Sintered copper-lead: not as slippery as babbitt, but good fatigue strength and load-carrying ability; fine for medium-duty use.

Cast copper-lead: the super-heavy-duty material. It has the highest fatigue strength and load-carrying ability. A nickel barrier of 30 to 50 millionths of an inch separates the babbitt outer layer from the cast copper-lead, to prevent a metallurgical combination of the two layers, which would destroy them both.

Choosing a replacement bearing actually is easy. When in doubt, buy the next heavier-duty bearing; it won't cost much more. On older cars, the sintered copper-lead is adequate. On late-model cars with up to medium powered engines, the aluminum alloy design will do. On high-performance engines, buy the cast copper-lead.

Installation of replacement bearings certainly isn't in the category of minor tuneup, but it is not a job that is necessarily out of the question for the weekend mechanic. To decide whether or not it's a job you can do, check to see how the oil pan comes

A A bearing shell is a multi-layer part. Outer layer is soft babbitt; backing is steel. One or two layers in between vary according to manufacturer and load-carrying needs.

out, as this is the part of the job that can be the most "brutish."

If part of the front suspension must be dropped to take out the oil pan, the job is going to be quite difficult under backyard conditions. The trouble comes when you try to bolt everything back in place, as it gets difficult to line up things.

If you have a pair of small hydraulic jacks (which sell for about $10 each) you can use them to keep the front suspension jacked up, and to assist in realigning everything when the job is ready to go back together. You'll definitely need a helper for the job.

If the engine has to be jacked up off its mounts to provide clearance for pulling the oil pan, another potential difficulty exists. You will need a floor jack to lift the engine, and probably a pair of safety stands to brace the engine in place. If you've got this equipment in your garage, you may be able to get the pan off. Once the job is

How to Change Engine Bearings

done, the engine has to be raised off the safety stands (which then are removed) onto the hydraulic jack. You'll need a helper with a crowbar at this point. One man jockeys the engine up and down with the jack, while the other moves it from side to side with the crowbar, until everything lines up. It sounds difficult and often it is. The whole operation takes but a few minutes under favorable conditions, longer when conditions get tough.

The best situation is when the oil pan can be dropped simply by unbolting it and lowering it from the engine. In this case, the job is substantially easier. The category that your car fits into depends on engine, car model and year, and any breakdown would fill this book. A careful perusal of the car underbody and the engine compartment should tell you how easy or difficult oil pan removal is.

Once the pan is off, the bearing caps, bolted in place, are in plain view and usually quite accessible. Just unbolt a cap, and you've got half a bearing in your hand.

If you're trying to replace main bearings, insert a roll-out pin (which can be bought for pennies or made from a cotter pin) into the crankshaft oil hole. Turn the crank by hand and the other half of the bearing will be rolled out.

Removing a connecting rod bearing is even easier. Unbolt the cap to remove one half, and push the rod away from the crankshaft to provide clearance to pull out the second half.

Now the critical part. If the crankshaft journal is smooth, and the bearing itself is merely well worn, installation of new bearings poses no problem. If, however, the crankshaft journals are scored, installation of new bearing shells will eliminate knocks and improve oil pressure only temporarily. If only one journal is bad, it may pay to have it ground smooth with the engine in the car. This is expensive, perhaps $25 or more for a single journal, but for just one

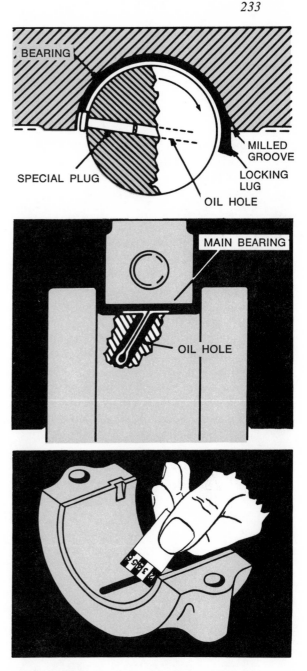

▲ Top: Main bearings can be removed and replaced without taking out the crankshaft. Simple way is to use roll-out pins, which have a stem that fits into crankshaft journal oil hole and a head that rolls the bearing shell in or out. Middle: Cotter pin can be bent to serve as roll-out pin. Above: Checking bearing clearance with Plasti-Gage determines whether undersize bearings are needed.

journal it's a lot cheaper and easier than pulling and dismantling the engine, and taking the crankshaft out. If a journal is ground, a standard size bearing will allow excessive clearance. You'll need an undersize bearing.

The most common situation is that some of the journals will have light scratches. In this case, installation of new bearings should prove worthwhile. There will be the elimination of knocks and improvement in oil pressure. And if a quality oil and oil filter are used, the bearing job should last long enough to pay for itself.

Important: Crankshaft and connecting-rod bearings must be precisely tightened, using a torque wrench (available for $10 to $12). Ask for the tightening specifications (given in foot-pounds) where you buy your bearings. There will be different specifications for connecting-rod and main bearings.

A common consideration is crankshaft journal wear. If the journals are worn more than about .002-inch, undersize bearings should be used. As a practical matter, however, if the journals are smooth, you can be sure they haven't worn significantly, and standard size replacement bearings can be used.

If you want to check, there are two ways. One is the use of Plasti-Gage, available in most auto parts houses. It consists of strips of plastic and permits very accurate measurement of bearing clearances. The plastic is laid across the bearing, which then is tightened to specifications and removed. The plastic will have been squashed to a certain width, which corresponds to a bearing clearance.

Another way is by use of a piece of feeler strip of desired thickness. Normally, the clearance with new bearing shells should be less than .004-inch (.001 to .002-inch is desirable). Get an .004 (or thinner) strip that is a bit less than the width of the bearing, and no more than a half-inch for its other dimension. Lay the strip so that the half-inch dimension is lengthwise. Torque the bearing to specifications and try to rock the crank (just an inch or so—no more). If the crank moves easily, undersize bearings are in order. If it locks completely or drags, install stand-size bearings.

The whole job, under favorable conditions, is a one-day project, and if you do it yourself, you should save at least a $75 labor charge. P.W.

See also: ENGINE; OIL, ENGINE.

▼ *Crankshaft journals should be mirror-smooth.*

Build These Bunk Beds

This double-deck bunk is an attractive space-saver with a design that any amateur carpenter can handle

THE BEDROOM FURNITURE pictured here is designed to take all the punishment an active youngster can dish out. And no matter how small the room, each of the pieces creates practical space for the many activities a young life requires.

The bunks are made with plywood. Their lines are graceful, yet simple enough to be built by any amateur home carpenter. The bunk beds are equipped with casters, so they can be rolled out from the wall to facilitate making the beds and mopping the floor behind them.

The bunks take standard 38 x 74-inch mattresses, known as twin size, which rest on ¼-inch plywood panels supported by a slat frame. The general appearance is very attractive, with the almost free-form double-Y supports painted in a dark color with semi-gloss enamel, while the beds themselves are retained in the clean natural birch color, smoothly finished with a clear coating.

First step is to make the yoke-shaped bunk support from ¾-inch plywood. Four parts A, and four parts B are needed. From one of your panels you can get three of the A parts and two of the B parts. The other three pieces can be cut from the second panel. This is an interesting and precise part of the work in which four separate parts are overlapped and joined to form each end support with a sturdy 1½-inch thickness.

The A parts are just 6½-inches wide across the center line, the B parts are just 14½-inches across the center line. Make a cardboard pattern for each by following the contours shown in the drawing on ruled 2-inch squares. Use a large enough cardboard so it can be folded over at the center line to give you the full-size pattern when it is opened up. Lay out the two patterns to obtain the five parts (listed above) on a single plywood panel, and the three additional parts from the second panel. The legs of all eight parts should be identical in contour.

For assembly, place an A and B part together, side by side, so that the edges of the wide flanges touch. On top, place a B part over the A part underneath, and the

▲ *The A and B parts (see drawing) for the double Y-shaped bunk supports are cut from two ³/₄"x4'x8' fir plywood panels, as shown.*

▲ *The support sections are joined to form a 1¹/₂" thick completed unit. The accompanying drawing shows details for making the joint.*

A part over the B. In that way, there is a natural overlap of the flanges. The drawing clearly shows how the parts overlap and join. Spread glue over the areas that will be joined, then fasten with wood screws into countersunk drilled pilot holes. Fill the screwhead holes with wood dough. Sand the edges of the entire unit so the two joined parts are smooth and continuous. A drum-type sanding tool will produce a neat result.

For beveling the edges of the supports, a router will give the best results in quickest time. You can use a bullnose cutter or other shaper bit to get the desired shape, though a satisfactory bevel can be obtained

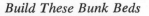

▲ *Putting the finishing touches on a completed support. You may want to paint support at this time.*

▲ *The floor frames are made of 1x2" pine strips 37¹/₂" long, spaced as shown and attached to two side pieces of 1x2" solid stock.*

Build These Bunk Beds 237

▲ Bunk sides (C) and ends (D) are cut to plan size and shape shown in the drawing. Assembly utilizes glue and brads.

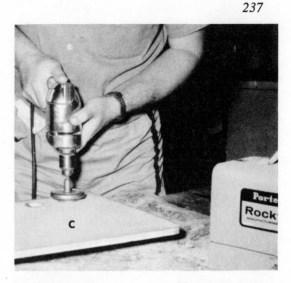

▲ Use a hole saw to drill 1³/₄-inch-diameter holes in sides of bunks. Holes should all be on a uniform level.

with a hand file. This should be used with care to avoid lifting the surface veneers. You may want to paint the supports the desired color at this time so that they will be dry and ready to use by the time the rest of the project is completed.

Drill the bottom leg ends for casters of the required size. Cut eight bunk blocks

from solid pine stock or ³/₄-inch plywood and attach them to the supports with #8, 1¼-inch oval head screws, at the positions shown in the drawing.

The bunks are built from ½-inch birch plywood. Select the best-looking grained side for the outside. Cut the sides (Part C) to a 13½-inch width and an 80-inch

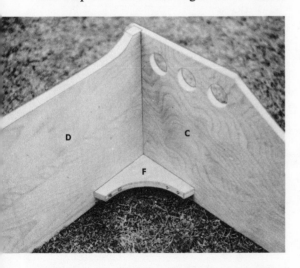

▲ Corner braces (F) strengthen assembly of sides and ends of bunk frames. Cleats (1x2") are also added to ends between corner braces.

▲ The assembled bunk, with floor frames attached to bunk sides with #8/1" screws. Bunk bottom of ¹/₄" fir plywood completes assembly.

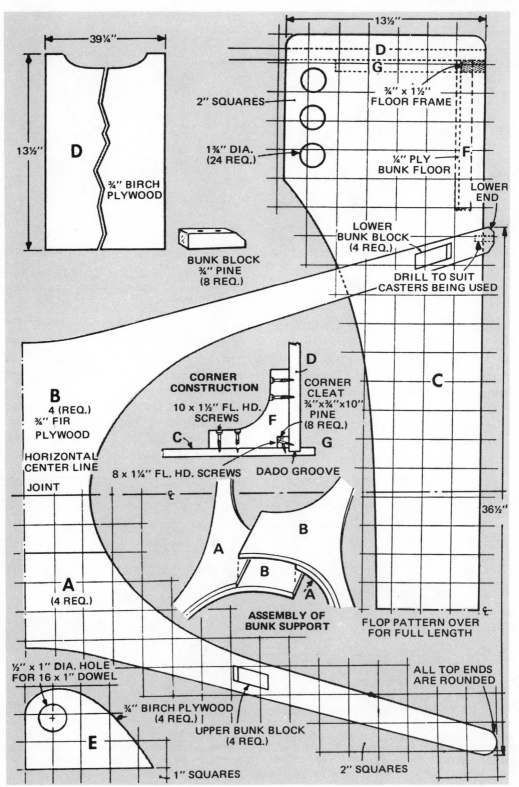

39¼″

13½″

D

¾″ BIRCH PLYWOOD

BUNK BLOCK ¾″ PINE (8 REQ.)

13½″

D

G

¾″ × 1½″ FLOOR FRAME

2″ SQUARES

1¾″ DIA. (24 REQ.)

¼″ PLY BUNK FLOOR

F

LOWER END

LOWER BUNK BLOCK (4 REQ.)

DRILL TO SUIT CASTERS BEING USED

B
4 (REQ.)
¾″ FIR PLYWOOD

HORIZONTAL CENTER LINE

JOINT

D

CORNER CONSTRUCTION

10 × 1½″ FL. HD. SCREWS

CORNER CLEAT ¾″×¾″×10″ PINE (8 REQ.)

C

F

G

8 × 1¼″ FL. HD. SCREWS

DADO GROOVE

C

36½″

B

A

B

B

A

A
(4 REQ.)

ASSEMBLY OF BUNK SUPPORT

FLOP PATTERN OVER FOR FULL LENGTH

½″ × 1″ DIA. HOLE FOR 16 × 1″ DOWEL

¾″ BIRCH PLYWOOD (4 REQ.)

UPPER BUNK BLOCK (4 REQ.)

ALL TOP ENDS ARE ROUNDED

E

1″ SQUARES

2″ SQUARES

length. All four sides can be obtained from the one 4 x 8-foot panel. Cut dado grooves, ¾-inch wide, near each end to receive the box ends. Shape the sides as shown, using a saber saw, and round off the corners. Drill 1¾-inch holes along the top, using a hole saw in a regular electric drill. Make sure the holes are all on a uniform level.

Cut the box ends (Part D) to size from ¾-inch birch plywood. Four ends are needed. Join the ends into the mortise grooves of the sides, assembling them with glue and brads. Countersink the nailheads and cover with wood dough. Long pipe clamps will help get a strong glued joint for these ends.

Make eight corner braces (Part F) and attach one at each corner of the bunk assembly with glue and #10, 1½-inch flathead screws. Assemble two floor frames, made of 1 x 2-inch solid stock. There are two pieces on the outside, each 64 inches long. Strips of the 1 x 2 stock, each 37½ inches long, are set between the outside lengths and spaced 13 inches apart on center, starting 6 inches from each end. There thus will be five cross strips. Join the strips to the outside lengths with glue and 6d finishing nails.

Attach a 1 x 2 cleat (part G) inside the bunk box at each end, between the corner braces, attached to the bunk ends with 1¼-inch screws. The cleats should be flush with the floor frame when it is set into place and attached to the bunk sides with #8, 1-inch flathead screws. This completes the bunk assembly, except for the floor of ¼-inch plywood which is cut to fit snug over the floor frame.

Make the ladder rung brackets (Part E) from ¾-inch birch plywood. Drill blind holes ½-inch deep for the 1-inch dowel rungs, assemble and attach to each end of the bunks.

When assembling the entire unit, rest the bunks on the support blocks, then fasten the bunks permanently with #10, 2-inch flathead countersunk screws through the bunk ends into the vertical support arms.

Original design by Steve Ellingson.

See also: HAND TOOLS; POWER TOOLS; LUMBER; ADHESIVES; WOODWORKING.

MATERIALS LIST		
Quantity	**Size and Description**	**Purpose**
2	³/₄″ 4′x8′ fire plywood (1 side good)	bunk supports
2	¹/₄″ 4′x8′ fir plywood (shop grade)	bunk bottoms
1	¹/₂″ 4′x8′ birch veneer plywood (1 side good)	bunk sides
1	³/₄″ 4′x5′ birch veneer plywood	bunk ends and corner braces
1	1″ hardwood dowel	ladder rungs
4 rolls	1″ flexible birch edge trim veneer and contact cement	covering exposed plywood edges
as needed	1″x2″ solid pine	bunk floor frame and cleats
as needed	#8 1¼″ flathead wood crews	
as needed	#8 1″ flathead wood screws	
as needed	#10 1½″ flathead wood screws	
as needed	#10 2″ flathead wood screws	
as needed	#8 1¼″ ovalhead wood screws	
NOTE: Also need, finishing nails, plastic resin glue, sandpaper, wood filler dough and paint.		

Race Car Bed

This easy-to-build child's bed looks like a racing car — and you can make it look as authentic as you wish with paint and decals

To MAKE IT "run," just add one child and a dream. Here is a bedmobile you can create that's sure to make "Bedtime!" an irresistible call to the young set.

It looks for all the world like a sleek racing car, and you can make it as authentic as you want by adding crossed checker flag decals, and others available at auto supply stores.

Built principally of plywood, the bedmobile is of sturdy construction, and it takes a standard size mattress. The hot-looking wheels are there for appearance only, the bed actually rests on a strong frame with casters.

Start by making a pattern on kraft paper and then transferring the pattern to the stock. Use ¾-inch plywood for the frame, and ½-inch plywood for the outer sides. Note that the same pattern is used for the frame sides and the outer sides, but that the dotted lines mark the limits of the frame sides. Use a power saber saw to cut out all the curved pieces. Clamp the four side pieces together for final trimming

and sanding to insure perfectly matched surfaces.

Assemble the front and rear frame members to the two frame side pieces, using glue and 8d finishing nails. Bevel the top edges of the front and rear members to match the curve of the sides. Cut out and install the two pairs of ¾-inch plywood stiffeners, then add the two outer sides. The basic form of the "car" is now apparent.

Three ¾-inch plywood cross pieces are made up. These are 2½ inches wide, 38 inches long; cut a 1½-inch deep by ¾-inch notch in the upper edge of each. Use 1½-inch x ¾-inch plywood for side, front, and rear ledges. Their location depends on the depth of the mattress, or mattress and box spring combination, you will use. Install the ledges and cross pieces with glue and 4d finishing nails. A mattress floor of ⅛-inch tempered hardboard is installed on top of the these members.

Turn the assembly upside down, and install the ¾-inch plywood mounting blocks at each corner, with glue and 2-inch #8 flathead wood screws. Be sure to countersink for the screws. Distance of the mounting blocks from the bottom edge of the bed is determined by the type of casters to be used, and the type of rug on the floor, if a rug is used. Clearance between the bed and a hard floor should be ½-inch, and at least ¾-inch between the bed and most carpets. A very thick pile rug will require even more distance.

Next add the center support member and cross strips that give shape to the front of the car. Cut the topside "skin" of ⅛-inch plywood slightly oversize to allow for trimming, and install it on the assembly. Start by fastening across the top

of the front frame member with glue and 2d finishing nails, then work back along the sides, and finally along the front edges. Cut extra strips to complete the topside over the rear wheels. Trim the topside flush with the sides and front, and round all edges with a file and sandpaper.

Cut out the panel that covers the underside of the front end; its three access holes are for retrieving any toys or other items that slip in the front end. At this stage it is advisable to paint the inside surfaces of all the front end members, then secure the panel with glue and 2d finishing nails. A flat black is recommended, and it also can be used on the outside surfaces of the inner side panels.

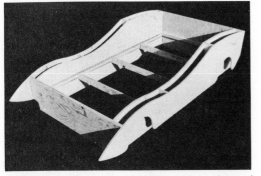

Basic form of car is apparent as plywood sides are attached. Stiffeners between frame and sides keep the latter rigid.

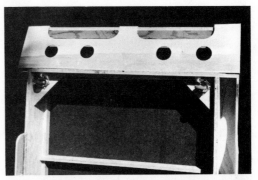

Underside of bed shows installed casters and mounting blocks. The clearance between bed and a hard floor must be ½-inch.

Wheels are a layup of 4 plywood discs, 3 of ¾-inch plywood and 1 of ½-inch plywood.

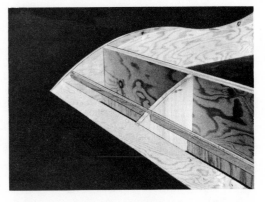

View of front end construction before top deck is installed.

Now make up the wheels. These are laminations of three ¾-inch plywood discs and one ½-inch plywood disc. Cut an inner circle in one of the ¾-inch discs to form the outside of the "tire." Use a tin or plastic plate, pie pan, or pot lid for the wheel itself—anything with a diameter of 5 to 6 inches. Round the edges of each tire for an authentic appearance. Make up the spinners and install with ¼-inch x 5-inch lag screw and flat washers.

Paint the bed the color or colors of your choice. Add racing stripes and numbers, and decals. With mattress, pillow, linens, and spread, it's ready for bedtime.

Original design by Steve Ellingson.

See also: HAND TOOLS; POWER TOOLS; WOOD-WORKING; PAINT; ADHESIVES.

MATERIALS LIST		
Quantity	**Size and Description**	**Purpose**
1	³/₄″ 4′x8′ fir plywood	frame
1	³/₄″ 4′x4′ fir plywood	frame, crosspieces, etc.
1	¹/₂″ 4′x8′ fir plywood	sides, wheels
1	¹/₈″ 4′x8′ Philippine mahogany plywood	skin
1	¹/₈″ 4′x8′ tempered hardboard	mattress floor
as needed	¹/₄″ scrap plywood	spinners
as needed	#8 2″ flathead wood screws	
4	¹/₄″x4″ lag screws with flat washers	
NOTE: Also need, glue, finishing nails, paint, decals, casters, wheel decoration.		

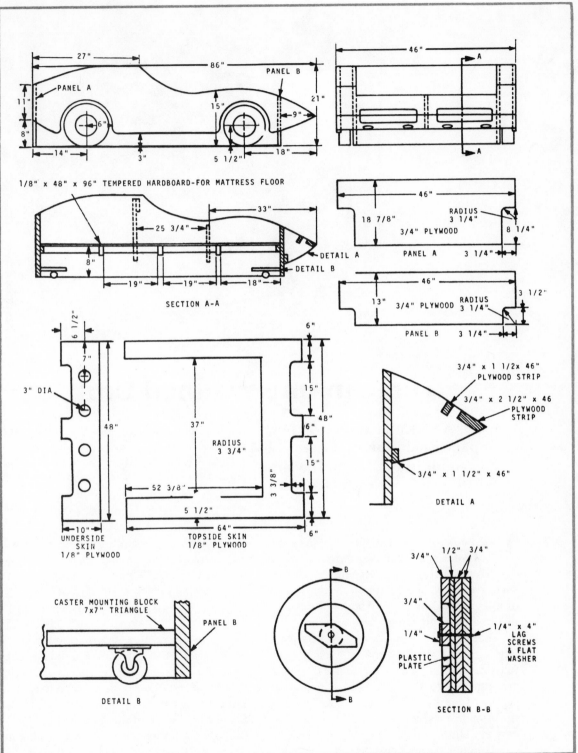

1/8" x 48" x 96" TEMPERED HARDBOARD-FOR MATTRESS FLOOR

SECTION A-A

PANEL A

PANEL B

DETAIL A

DETAIL B

UNDERSIDE SKIN 1/8" PLYWOOD

TOPSIDE SKIN 1/8" PLYWOOD

CASTER MOUNTING BLOCK 7x7" TRIANGLE

PANEL B

DETAIL B

SECTION B-B

Three-in-one Wallbed Unit

A versatile and attractive space-saver, this unit is easily built from plywood, using ordinary tools

THE BEDROOM planned just for sleeping is wasted space for two-thirds of each day. Here's a way to use less furniture in a small room and still retain all the functions of a bigger bedroom set. The handsome 3-in-1 wallbed unit shown here requires only the space of one twin-size bed, yet its four large drawers give you the equivalent of a full-size dresser. The wall shelves, which are attached to the bed, hold a generous supply of books and knickknacks. The entire unit is mounted on heavy casters for easy mobility.

All major components are of plywood;

the unit pictured is of birch plywood, but you can use any veneer of your choice. Exposed plywood edges can be painted to contrast with the natural-finished wood surfaces, or you can cover the edges with matching flexible wood tape for a truly professional finish.

For such a large unit, the construction is relatively simple, and no special tools are needed although a power saw speeds and simplifies cutting out the various parts.

Start by cutting the front panel from ¾-inch plywood. Make the cut-outs for the four drawers and cupboard drawer. Trim all edges so they are smooth and square with the surface. Make up two drawer slide frames. These have scalloped end pieces; you can clamp the four end pieces together when cutting and trimming the scallops for an exact match. These scallops are more than decorative—particularly as they are inside the unit—as screw holes must be drilled through the center of each scallop.

Assemble the two drawer slide frames with glue and #6 2½-inch flathead wood screws, then attach the two frames to the back of the front panel, as shown in the photo. Use glue, and #6 1¾-inch flathead wood screws inserted through the frame

screw holes and driven into the front panel. Attach corner cleats at each end of the front panel with glue and #6 1¼-inch screws.

Cut out the two end pieces, and notch the upper rear corner of each as shown on the plans. Fasten these to the front panel with glue and #6 1½-inch flat head wood screws. These are driven through the end

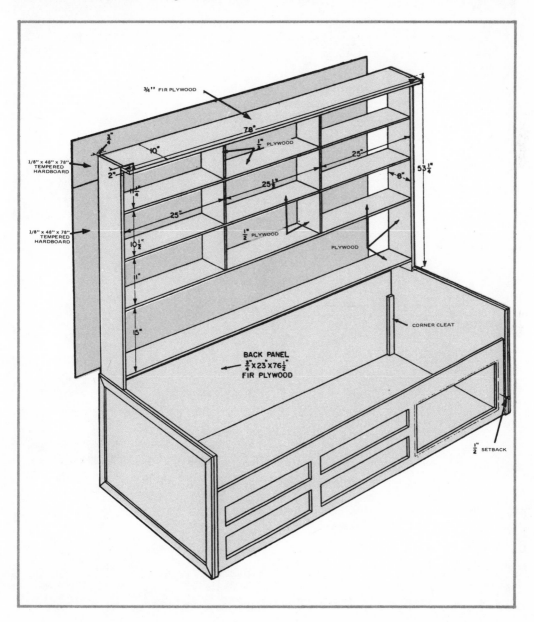

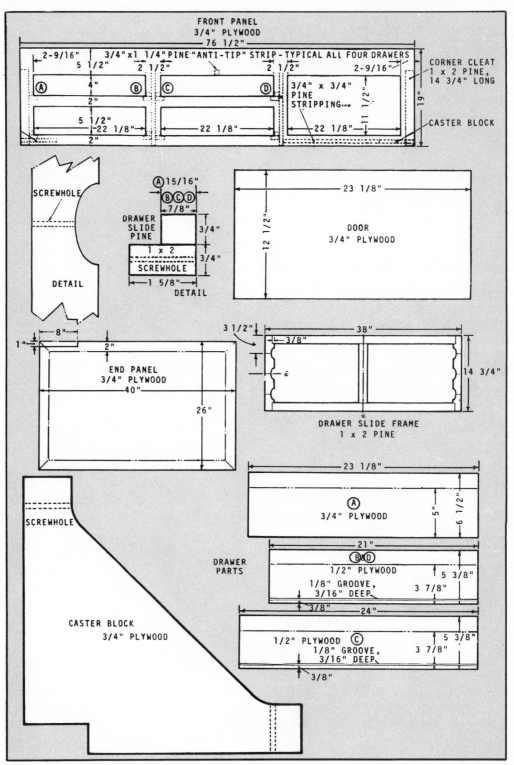

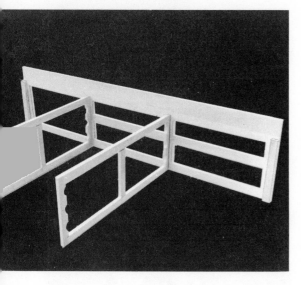

◄ *Assembled drawer side frames are attached to back of front panel with glue and flathead wood screws.*

▼ *View of right front corner as you stand behind bed. Note support block for "anti-tip" strip of lower drawer.*

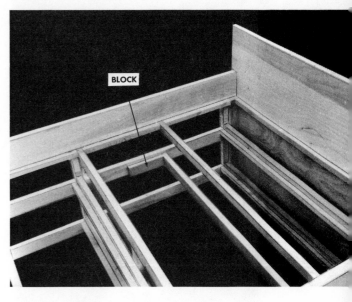

BLOCK

panels into the cleats. Be sure to drill and countersink for all screws. These screw heads are later covered by trim pieces. Cut out and attach the back panel, using corner cleats in the same manner as on the front panel. Attach the drawer slide frames to the back panel at this time. Work carefully, and make sure that everything is perfectly square!

Make up eight drawer slides from 1 x 2-inch and 1 x 1-inch pine stock, as shown on the plans. The assembled slides are fastened to the drawer slide frames with #6 1¾-inch flathead wood screws. Install the ¾ x ¾-inch pine stripping all around the frame. Install the two "anti-tip" strips for the drawers. The lower one nails to a block that is glued and screwed to the front panel.

Now install the cupboard support strip, caster blocks, and the stripping for the cupboard floor. Use glue and #6 1¾-inch flathead wood screws for the caster blocks, and glue and finishing nails for the support strip. Cut the cupboard wall and floor from ⅛-inch tempered hard board, trim to fit, and install with finishing nails. Add outer trim to the end panels. This can be ½ x 2-inch matching plywood, or hardwood or mold-

ing of your choice. Install with glue and finishing nails. Set the nail heads and fill with plastic wood.

The basic bed framework is completed by adding the mattress floor panel. This is nailed to the upper stripping. Cut out the cupboard drawer, and trim it so that it overlaps the frame opening by ½-inch on all sides. Add hinges, catch, and door handle of your choice.

Make up the four drawers next. A ⅛-inch wide groove, ³⁄₁₆-inch deep, is cut along the bottom of the "B" and "C" panels. When front, back, and sides are assembled with glue and finishing nails, the bottoms of ⅛-inch tempered hardboard can be slid into these grooves. Glue and nail the bottom to the back piece "D" of each drawer.

Cut bookcase top, uprights, and shelves from ¾-inch plywood. Fasten ¾ x ¾-

◄ *Underside of bed. Note center support strip/ stripping to support cupboard floor. Use glue, finishing nails.*

STRIPPING

SUPPORT STRIP

▼ *All parts of ³/₄" plywood bookcase unit assembled. Note pine cleats used to hold lower shelf to uprights.*

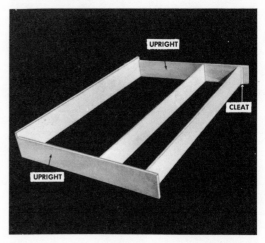

UPRIGHT

CLEAT

UPRIGHT

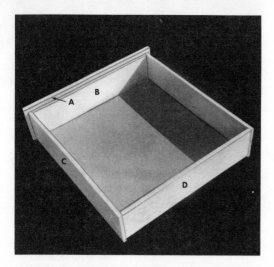

▲ *Completed drawer. When front, back and sides are assembled, hardboard bottoms can be slid into grooves.*

inch cleats to the uprights with glue and #6 1¼-inch flathead wood screw. Lower shelf is then attached to the cleats, and additional shelves are attached to the uprights, with glue and finishing nails. Use a temporary diagonal support to hold the work square while work is in progress, and add remaining shelves and dividers of ½-

inch plywood. Remove the diagonal strip, and attach the back of ⅛-inch tempered hardboard. Use glue and finishing nails.

Mount the bookcase on the bed unit, setting the uprights into the notches of the two side pieces. Fasten with screws through the uprights into the exterior trim strips that run along the top of the side panels. Screws through the hardboard back of the bookcase into the back panel of the bed give additional support.

Finally, paint all exposed plywood edges, or cover with flexible wood trim, then give the unit the finish of your choice. If you have picked a plywood with a decorative veneer such as birch, maple, or mahogany, you will want to use a varnish or other clear finish to bring out its beauty. Use at least two coats, and sand lightly between coats. Add drawer pulls and the door handle, mattress, and bedding.

Original design by Steve Ellingson.

See also: FURNITURE, INDOOR; HAND TOOLS; POWER TOOLS.

MATERIALS LIST

Quantity	Size and Description	Purpose
2	¾" 4'x8' hardwood plywood	bedframe and book-case members
1	½" 25"x8' hardwood plywood	bookcase shelves, dividers
1	¾" 4'x8' fir plywood	back panel, bookcase top, shelves
1	⅜" 4'x8' fir plywood	mattress floor panel
1	½" 4'x8' fir plywood	drawers
2	⅛" 4'x8' tempered hardboard	drawer bottoms, cup-board side and floor bookcase back
1	1" 2"x53" pine	drawer slide frames and slides
1	1" 1'x8' pine shelving	stripping, etc.
2	½"x1½" butt hinges	doors
4	swivel type casters, plate mounted, heavy duty, 2½" maximum height	Casters
as needed	#6 2½" flathead wood screws	
as needed	#6 1¾" flathead wood screws	
as needed	#6 1½" flathead wood screws	
as needed	#6 1¼" flathead wood screws	

NOTE: Also need, finishing nails, paint, Plastic Wood, glue and hardware.

What You Should Know about Bicycles

Bikes come in a multitude of shapes, sizes, models and styles. Here's how to pick out the one that meets your needs safely and practically

THE DEGREE to which you will enjoy cycling will depend largely on how wisely you select your bike. For some individuals an expensive 10-speed bicycle is a must, for others the same bike would be an extravagance. But there is one common denominator: the overriding importance of safety. So here are some tips to help you choose the most practical, and safest bicycle for your needs.

Types of bicycles. Basically you can think of adult-size bikes as either conventional middleweights, or lightweights. (In bicycling, an adult is any person who is large enough to ride a full-size bicycle; the bicycle industry considers anyone over age 14 as adult-sized.)

Within these two weight categories, you find bicycles of different styles that are suitable for specific riding purposes. Some are designed for moderate distance touring, while others are for long-distance touring; three-speed bikes are especially good for business commuters; middleweight models are best for local riding, as on newspaper delivery routes; adult three-wheelers are for those who have large loads to transport or for those whose sense of balance is not the best; folding bicycles facilitate transport in cars and boats; tandem bikes promote togetherness; one-wheeled models (unicycles) are for the adventurous and those having better-than-average balance.

The traditional bicycle made in the U.S. is a middleweight vehicle weighing 50 or 60 pounds. It has a coaster brake (the kind that operates when you push backward on the pedals) and relatively thick tires. It is relatively trouble-free and easy to maintain, and a good bike for such short-distance uses as delivering newspapers or for just funning around in your neighborhood.

Lightweight bicycles weigh as much as 15 pounds less than the middleweights. The lighter weight plus three speeds make this category of bicycle very popular as a general use bicycle among adults. Expect to pay as much as three times the cost of a middleweight vehicle.

There are still lighter bicycles weighing under 25 pounds that some view as a third basic category. These have anywhere from 5 to 15 gears, with 10 gears perhaps being the most popular. Other features include hand-lever brakes, dropped-down handle bars of the type seen on racing bicycles and thin, hard tires.

Who needs 15 gears? Relatively few cyclists need a bicycle having fifteen gears, but many riders will find five or ten gears useful. On the other hand, others would wonder why they spent money on extra gears when one—or at most three—gears would have sufficed.

The number of gears your bicycle should have should be determined largely in relation to the kind of terrain you expect to travel. Extra gears are used to maintain as consistent a pedaling rhythm as possible because for most individuals a cadence of 65 to 85 pedaling revolutions per minute is most comfortable. The trouble is that you just can't maintain this rpm when pedaling up a steep hill with a conventional single-speed bike. So you drop to a lower gear which requires less physical effort on your part. This means, of course, that you travel a shorter distance per pedal revolution, so you sacrifice speed for the sake of energy conservation. The general rule is that the steeper the slope you must climb, the lower the gear you use, and the slower you move ahead. You would also use a lower gear when bucking a heavy wind.

The higher gears are used primarily on down grades or when the wind is at your back. If you live in very flat country, you really have no use for a multi-speed bicycle, except perhaps as a status symbol. But if you will be touring through hilly country—New England, for example—you had better have at least five gears, maybe even ten. If you are setting out for the Colorado Rockies, or if you are planning some really long-distance touring, you might even want a 15 gear vehicle.

Gearing ratios on bicycles are listed as whole numbers. For example, "70" gear is used on bicycles intended for "normal" riding conditions. The number relates to the distance you travel during one revolution of the pedal crank. To calculate the

BICYCLE GEARING CHART

The following gearing information which applies to various models of one manufacturer's bicycles illustrates the relationships between gear numbers (see text) and the distance traveled during one revolution of the pedal crank. Note especially that even those 10-speed bikes having the same wheel size (diameter in inches) may have different gear ratios. This explains why the top-speed gear in one bike may move you ahead a bit faster than the top speed on another similar 10-speed cycle.

Wheel Size	No. of Speeds	Gear Range	Distance Range
26″	3	49-88	154-277
26″	5	37-85	116-251
27″	5	39-89	122-279
24″	10	33-89	104-279
27″	10	38-100	119-314
27″	10	33-100	104-314
27″	10	32-104	100-327
27″	10	51-100	160-314
27″	15	31-104	102-327

actual distance you multiply the gear number by "pi" which is the mathematical constant of 3.14 used to figure the circumference of a circle. In this example (70 x 3.14) you find that one revolution of the pedal crank will move you almost 220 inches or a little more than 18 feet. Bear in mind that different 10-speed bicycles that have the same wheel diameter may provide different gear ratios, hence different travel distance per pedal crank revolution.

There are two different systems for changing the gear ratios on a bicycle: a *variable gear hub* which utilizes a planetary gear set within the hub of the rear wheel (this system is commonly used on three- to five-speed bikes); and a *dérailleur* ("derailer") system which utilizes a mechanism that makes the chain mechanism jump from one sprocket to another. If you buy a 5-, 10- or 1.5-gear dérailleur bicycle, be prepared to spend a little time learning how to shift the gears smoothly; learning to ride such a bike requires more effort than you spent on the conventional

single-speed vehicle you prized as a child. You will find that most three-speed bikes have small finger levers near the hand grip to operate the gears, but at least one make now features a twist-grip gearshift control (you just twist one of the handles you grasp for steering).

Good brakes for safety. In your eagerness to take home a multi-speed bicycle, do not overlook the vital importance of choosing a bicycle having a good brake system. Your life could some day depend on how well the brake works.

We are all familiar with the traditional coaster brake. You just push the pedals in reverse to apply braking action. But chances are that you are now more interested in a bike having a so-called caliper brake which you operate by squeezing a lever near the hand grip. The lever actuates a mechanical linkage connected to each wheel and these in turn press small pads against the wheel rims. Caliper brakes can be operated faster and more easily than coaster brakes, but they do have one fault: braking action is likely to be different when

▷ *Dropped handlebars are used on touring and racing bicycles. They provide a nearly horizontal body position, which is less tiring over long distances and reduces wind resistance.*

FRAME SIZES FOR VARIOUS LEG LENGTHS

Leg length is the distance from the crotch to the floor while standing in stocking feet. Although a practical straddle test (see text) is vital, this table relating to 26″ and 27″ wheel size bicycles will help you zero in on the probable best frame size even before you visit a bicycle shop.

Frame Size (in inches)	Leg Length Range (in inches)
17	26 to 30
19	28 to 31
20	29 to 32
21	30 to 33
22	31 to 34
23	32 to 35
24	33 to 36
25	34 to 37
26	35 to 38

the wheel rim is dry than when it is wet (as during a rain or after you ride through a puddle). For an excellent, detailed evaluation of various caliper type braking systems consult the November 1972 issue of *Consumer Reports* which you can probably find at your local library.

The Food and Drug Administration's Bureau of Product Safety has determined that a particularly tricky-to-operate brake system is one consisting of a conventional coaster brake on the rear wheel and a caliper brake on the front wheel; the agency is pressing for elimination of such combination brakes, especially on bicycles used by youngsters.

Fit and adjustment are important. You cannot truly enjoy cycling, or engage in the activity safely, unless you choose a bicycle that fits your physical build and unless you make seat and handlebar adjustments properly.

Leading bicycle makers offer a variety of frame sizes so there is no good reason why you should settle for anything less than a perfect fit. If you are purchasing a man's bike, stand flat-footed on the floor

while straddling the horizontal bar; you should have from ½-inch to 1-inch of space between the bar and your inseam. Women's bicycles have no horizontal bar, so women should use a man's bicycle to determine the approximate correct frame size (wear slacks when you go bike shopping).

Bear in mind that the frame size is independent of the wheel size, although in any given frame size the seat will be closer to the ground on a 26-inch wheel bike than on a 27-inch model. If you find that you

⬆ *Straight handlebars allow the rider to remain nearly erect.*

can't properly straddle the smallest available frame on a 27-inch wheel bicycle, you may have to settle for a 26-inch wheel model. Be sure that the seat is at the lowest possible position when making such comparisons.

The straddle test is but the start. You must also make sure that your feet reach the pedals properly when you are seated. The most efficient and comfortable pedaling is accomplished if, when you are seated on the bicycle, your leg is *not quite* fully extended when the ball of your foot is on the pedal in the bottom position. Although some will say that your leg should be fully extended, you will probably find that a slight bend at the knee gives you a surer foot grip on the pedal. In any event, you can always raise the seat slightly to provide fuller leg extension if you find that preferable; but you can't make any such adjustment if you start with a full leg extension with the seat in its lowest position and you later decide that less leg extension would have been better.

After adjusting the seat to the most comfortable height for you, move it toward the front or rear so that the nose of the saddle (seat) is two inches or a little less from the centerline of the bottom bracket. If the seat has been correctly positioned, you should easily reach and grasp the handles when you lean forward about ten degrees. If you cannot meet this test, you may have to substitute a different stem on the handlebar to move the grips closer to

▲ *Horizontal-top frame bar should be about one inch lower than your inseam when you straddle the bar and stand on the ground.*

you, or further away if you have an unusually long reach. Moving the seat closer isn't always the best answer because you may not then have enough forward as well as downward thrust against the pedals. For maximum pedaling efficiency you should be seated a little behind the pedals, not directly above them.

The handlebar stem is usually adjusted to the same height as the seat, or slightly lower. Just remember that at least two inches of both the handlebar stem and the seat-post must remain inside the fork stem and frame after all adjustments are made to ensure adequate holding strength.

The same general procedures should be followed when selecting a bicycle for a youngster. It is especially important to observe the straddle test because a boy can hurt himself if he slips onto the horizontal bar without being able to check himself by planting his feet on the ground. Also be especially careful to avoid bicycles that have levers or other equipment mounted on the horizontal bar, too close to the seat. And be advised and guided by the fact that there is a move afoot to ban certain bicycles, especially those having inordinately high or weirdly shaped handlebars, that are known to be unsafe. Don't buy your child a hard-to-control bike—which may become a death machine—no matter how hard he pleads for the same kind of groovy bike his friends ride.

If your child is under 12 years old, look for a bike having a coaster brake. It may be old-fashioned in his (or her) eyes, but it would be much safer because children in the under-twelve age bracket usually do not have the arm reach and finger power to operate caliper brakes firmly. Above all, do not buy a bicycle having both coaster and caliper brakes, says the FDA.

Safe riding habits. There's more to riding a bicycle safely than merely staying upright and knowing how to operate the gearshift and brake. You must develop

---

FDA's EIGHT BICYCLE SAFETY RECOMMENDATIONS

In 1972, representatives of major bicycle manufacturers agreed to *consider* meeting the following safety recommendations proposed by the Food & Drug Administration's Bureau of Product Safety. When you shop for a bicycle, see which manufacturers have taken these consumer-benefiting proposals to heart:

1. Add light reflecting materials or devices to make bicycles visible in the dark *and* identifiable as bicycles.

2. Provide pedals having enough sliding friction to prevent rider's shoes from slipping.

3. Design and locate gearshifts and other devices located on the horizontal bars of boy's bikes so as to minimize risk of injury.

4. Limit seat post length to prevent raising seat to a height that would jeopardize good control of the bicycle.

5. Eliminate front-wheel caliper brakes from bicycles (particularly from juvenile bikes) equipped with rear-wheel coaster brakes.

6. Design caliper brake grips to accommodate the rider's handspan.

7. Eliminate all raw, sharp or rough metal edges on any parts, including handlebars for which grips are provided.

8. Apply industry safety standards to two-wheeled sidewalk bicycles and to bikes equipped with removable training wheels.

---

good riding habits if you are to remain alive while riding on highways that are filled with speeding cars. The basic rule is to adhere to the same general road rules that apply to autos; give clear hand signals before stopping (wave your arm in an up-and-down motion), indicate left and right turns, stop at red lights and at all intersections before proceeding. Do everything possible to remain visible to motorists; when the line of traffic stops, try to be where the motorist ahead of you can see you in his rear view mirror (suppose he suddenly backs up without knowing you are there?), and above all do not ride at night or even at dusk without lights.

Riding in city traffic is in many ways different from riding along suburban streets or on country roads. In the city, where there is considerable congestion, it is vital that you ride in a very straight line. Do not attempt to cope with city traffic until you are expert at straight line riding, even at very slow speeds. Always ride with the traffic, avoid sudden stops, and keep to the right but not right next to the curb or too close to parked cars (leave some maneu-

vering space in case of emergency). Stay alert to what people in parked cars are doing; if someone suddenly pulls out, or even opens a car door in your path, you could be seriously injured or even killed if you are diverted into the path of a following car.

If you ride to work or some other place regularly, plan a route that takes you through streets having the least traffic—even if it means riding a somewhat longer distance. And as a general rule, try to avoid streets where no parking of autos is permitted because these are very narrow streets, hence especially hazardous. There are exceptions, of course; you may actually be safest on a wide street where parking is banned for other reasons.

In the open country you must cope with somewhat different kinds of hazards. Perhaps the greatest danger derives from the much faster car speeds, so try to keep to one side of the road—especially in locations where following cars may not see you because of a sharp curve or other obstructions. Whether you should ride with the traffic flow, or against it as is proper for pedestrians, is still a point of controversy. However, the consensus seems to favor riding with the traffic because the speed ratio between you and a passing car is smaller if that car is catching up with you than if it is approaching you head on. For example, if you are travelling at a speed of 15 miles per hour, and a car approaching you head on is moving at 50 mph, a head-on collision would be the equivalent of hitting a solid object at a speed of 65

PROPER FRAME FIT

Rider MUST be able to straddle bicycle when standing

PROPER RIDER ADJUSTMENT

Handlebar stem approximately level with seat or slightly lower

Knee slightly bent

Pedal at bottom position

mph. But if the trailing car hits you, the impact is more in the order of 35 mph. It's quite a big difference. However, common sense will dictate when the basic rule of riding with the traffic should be broken; if crossing to the other side clearly makes you more visible to cars moving in both directions, then by all means do cross over.

Other country-riding rules you should observe include the following: avoid federal or state highways even if cycling is not specifically banned; be alert to motorists popping out of driveways (especially hidden driveways); approach and pass through intersections with care; watch out for dogs (if you are bitten, try to determine whose dog it was, or at least memorize the appearance of the dog, and seek medical help immediately even if the bite is only superficial).

Children should be taught all these same safe-riding rules. But they require some additional instruction. One of the worst juvenile riding habits is zipping out of a driveway, onto a suburban road, without stopping or looking both ways; you can see this happening daily in almost any suburban area. Make sure your child does not do this. Also make it very clear that you will not tolerate weaving, even in light traffic, or stunt riding on public highways. More than one rider on a one-person bike should be strictly forbidden. Be sure that the child's bicycle has a coaster brake, and that it is always in good condition. Also, to ensure good braking, see that tires are in good shape and properly inflated. Soft tires not only wear out faster, but, more importantly, they make proper handling of the bicycle much more difficult.   J.H.

See also: CAMPING; CAMPING EQUIPMENT.

GLOSSARY OF BICYCLE TERMS
Ankling. Technique of pedaling; foot puts pressure on the pedal all the way around the stroke.

Bottom bracket. A round tube containing

What You Should Know about Bicycles

▲ *When buying children's bikes, avoid exaggerated heights in seats and handlebars for safety's sake. Also, avoid a bike with a coaster brake for rear wheel and a caliper brake for front one. This combination is dangerous.*

the axle for the chain wheel and cranks. The seat tube, down tube and stays are welded to the bottom bracket.

Brake levers. Handlebar levers used to operate caliper brakes.

Cable. Any wire leading to caliper brakes or to derailleur gears.

Caliper brakes. Hand operated brakes that slow down or stop a bike by pressing pads against the wheel rims.

Chain. The articulated drive belt which transmits power from the chain wheel to the rear wheel.

Chain stays. Frame tubes connecting the bottom bracket to the point where the rear wheel fits into the frame.

Chain wheel. The large geared wheel on the right side of the bottom bracket that engages the chain.

Coaster brakes. Internal hub rear brakes actuated by pushing foot pedals in reverse.

Cranks. The steel or aluminum members to which pedals are reached; the right side crank is attached to the chain wheel and the left side crank is attached to the axle.

Cyclometer. A device that measures traveled mileage.

Derailleur. A device which moves the chain from one gear to another in one type of multi-speed bike. This is a French word meaning "derailer." See also variable gear hub.

Derailleur cage. Unit holding rear derailleur idler wheels.

Dishing. Technique of truing a derailleur gear-equipped rear wheel so that the rim is centered over the axle. A properly dished wheel appears to be to the right of hub center, on the gear side. Also called truing.

Down tube. The frame member connecting the steering head and bottom bracket.

258

Drop outs. Section of the front fork where the wheel or hub axle fits and to which the wheel axle is bolted; the same section where the rear chain stays are located.

Fork crown. Flat or sloping section at the top of the fork, just under the steering head.

Front fork. The two forklike bars leading to the hub of the front wheel. The fork is turned by the handlebars to effect steering. This unit includes the steering-column fork crown inside the head tube of the frame, the fork tips, and the fork blades which are round or oval depending on whether the bike is for track or road use.

Front drop out. A lug brazed to the front fork bottom tips. The front wheel axle fits into this lug.

Gearing. A whole number that relates the distance traveled to one revolution of the pedal crank.

Handlebar stem. A steel or dural member connecting the handlebars to the steering head.

Headset. See steering head.

Hub. Front or rear wheel unit containing the axle and bearings; includes holes to which spokes are attached.

Jockey sprocket. Top of two rear derailleur idler wheels; used to move the chain from one gear to another.

Mudguards. Fenders.

Mudguard stays. Braces holding the fenders in place.

Pannier. Bags for carrying clothing and other supplies. Some attach to the rear of the bicycle, usually in pairs for better balance, while others are designed for front mounting.

Quick-release skewer. Special mechanism that permits removal of front and rear wheels in seconds.

Randonneur handlebars. One type of dropped handlebars that allow several hand positions. Other similar dropped handlebars used for road touring and

racing are the Maes road bars and Pista track racing handlebars.

Rattrap pedals. All-steel racing and touring pedals.

Rear drop out. Lug into which rear axle fits.

Rim. Wheel member to which the tire is attached.

Saddle. Seat.

Seat cluster. A three-way lug joining the top tube, seat tube and seat stays.

Seat post. Tube to which the seat is attached; fits into seat tube.

Seat stays. Section of frame exending from just under the seat to the rear wheel drop out.

Seat tube. A frame member under the seat which is fastened to the bottom bracket and to the top tube.

Skewer. A quick-release device permitting removal of the wheel for fast repair of flats; used on racing type wheel hubs.

Steering head. Tube containing fork cups and bearings, the stem and the top section of the fork. Also called the headset.

Stem. The handlebar stem (gooseneck) that fits into the steering head to hold the handlebars in place.

Tension roller. Bottom of two rear derailleur idler wheels; keeps correct tension on the chain.

Tire, clincher. A heavy tire having a wire bead on the edge and a removable tube.

Tire, tubular. Light touring or racing tire. Clincher and tubular tires are not interchangeable on the same rim.

Toe clips. Cage on pedals.

Top tube. Frame member running from the steering head to the seat tube.

Truing. Another term for dishing.

Valve. Metal tube attached to tire through which air is pumped into the tire.

Variable gear hub. A rear hub containing from two to five internal gears and as many gear ratios to effect speed changes. Shifting is done by means of a lever mounted on the handlebars.

How to Fix Bicycles

Bike boom + bike shortage = do-it-yourself

Today, when dealers can't seem to get enough new lightweight bicycles to meet demand, the proper maintenance of your old bicycle is more important than ever before. If you haven't got a bike, don't be afraid to buy a used one. You can overhaul it and join this fast growing sport.

A popular type of adult bicycle is the three-speed English lightweight tourist bike, often called, incorrectly, "English racer." European-made bikes, imported by some department stores, are similar in construction. Because of wide ownership, these bikes are frequently available in the used trade from bike shops or at giveaway prices from neighborhood garage sales. They are the Falcons and Valiants of the bicycle world; not quite as sporty as the ten-speeds, but far superior to the ordinary child's heavyweight. And they use parts and tires that are inexpensive and easy to find. As long as it's not rusted out or completely inoperative, you should be able to overhaul any bike you buy. Give it a test drive to be sure nothing is frozen stiff.

The only special tools that you will need are a spoke wrench, which costs about 35 cents, and a thin end-wrench to fit the wheel cones and pedals of your particular bike. An ordinary bicycle wrench will probably do the job. If it doesn't fit, buy a cheap end-wrench of the proper size and grind off one side of the jaws until it is thin enough to squeeze between a wheel cone and locknut. For other parts an adjustable wrench and a pair of water pump pliers will substitute for a whole tool kit.

Parts, if needed, can be purchased at your local bike shop, department store, or discount mart. While all parts of a bicycle need routine maintenance, those that contribute most to a free running bike are the wheels, chain, bottom bracket bearings, and pedals. Let's begin with the front wheel.

Remove the wheel from the fork; then back off the locknut and cone at one end of the axle. Remove the axle and bearings. English bikes have loose ball bearings, so a newspaper should be spread below the wheel to catch the balls. Clean the parts in kerosene and inspect them. Replace any

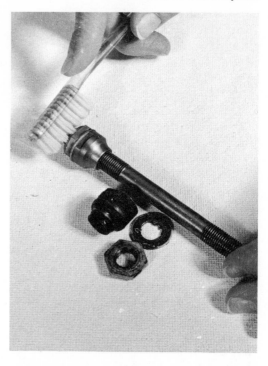

▲ Tools needed include (l. to r., above) spoke and bike wrenches, old toothbrush, cycle lube, marking crayon, adjustable pliers and crescent wrench. After removing front axle and bearings, scrub cones with toothbrush dipped in kerosene (right). Note gunk on uncleaned cone, nut and washer. Replace where necessary. ➤

bearings that show rust or pitting. Lubricate the hub with bicycle grease or any general purpose grease, and stick the ball bearings in the grease. Cover the bearings with more grease, and re-install the axle, cones, washers and locknuts. Tighten the cones against the bearings, then back off a cone about ¼ turn. The wheel should spin freely, but the axle should have no end play. Tighten the locknuts, if present, against the cones to hold the adjustment. On some bikes the cones fit tightly into the fork, and the outside nut locks the assembly.

Mount the wheel in the fork, and check it with chalk or crayon for out-of-roundness. Loosen spoke nipples where the rim radius is short, tighten them where it is long. Then check for side-to-side wobble. Loosen spokes from one side of the hub and tighten those from the other side to remove lateral "bumps." Cut out and replace rusty spokes that defy adjustment, but to avoid error replace one spoke at a time. Check the nipples in the rims for

protruding spoke ends after adjustment. File off any long ends to protect your tube.

The rear wheel should also be trued, if necessary, and checked for bearing adjustment. But the rear hub should be dismantled only if it fails to operate and if you have a diagram of your particular unit. Three-speed hubs require periodic lubrication with SAE #20 motor oil and occasional adjustment of the indicator spindle. Frequently, a sluggish unit will gradually respond to nothing more than a good oiling plus use.

To release the chain, locate the master link and pry off the keeper. Soak the chain in kerosene to remove dirt and old grease or oil. Oil with SAE #20 motor oil and hang up to drain. Or use a special lubricant for chains. If your chain has no master link, brush it with a toothbrush dipped in kerosene, then wipe dry. Lubricate it lightly in place.

Set the bike upside down on the saddle and handlebar. Turn the pedals and cranks

How to Fix Bicycles

and listen closely. With the chain off the chain wheel, the bottom bracket should be quiet. Any clicking or grinding noise indicates dry bearings or gritty grease which should be replaced.

English and European bikes usually have three-piece cranksets which come apart for servicing. To remove the cranks, prepare a block of wood to support the crank and receive the tapered crank pins. Drill a ⅜-inch hole into one end of a 28-inch length of 2x4. The hole should be as close as possible to one edge. Back off the nuts on the pins and drive out the pins as shown in photo. Make note of the direction in which the tapered pin was inserted through the crank.

Pull off the cranks and pedals. Turn the bike on its right side to get at the left side of the bottom bracket. Loosen the lock ring, use a hammer and punch if necessary, and remove it. Remove the left ball cup, bearings, and axle. Use a newspaper to catch the loose balls, usually 11 on each side. Wash the parts in kerosene and inspect. Clean the inside of the bracket. The

▲ Replace front wheel in fork and check for trueness by holding a crayon near the outside of rim and spinning the wheel. Wobbly wheel will pick up crayon marks.

▲ After checking rim for up and down wobble, use spoke wrench to loosen nipples where rim radius is short or tighten where it's long. Then check for side-to-side wobble.

▲ Clean hub and apply bicycle grease. Pack cleaned or new bearings in grease, install and adjust by tightening cone against bearing, then backing off ¼ turn.

right cup has a left hand thread and need not be removed unless it has been damaged.

Put new grease in the cups and install the clean, or new, bearings. Cover the balls with grease and install the axle, left cup, and lock ring. The long end of the axle should be on the right to hold the chain wheel. Tighten until the axle binds, then back off the cup about ¼ turn. Test for end play versus binding, and lock it in proper adjustment with the lock ring.

Check the pedals for noise or binding. If your bike has pedals with a removable dust cap on the outside end, you can dismantle them. Remove the dust caps, the locknut, the washer, and the axle cone. Hold the pedal axle itself in place until you have removed and counted the outside balls. Then pull out the axle and inside balls. Most pedals have more balls in the inside end of the pedal than in the outside end. Wash, grease, and replace the parts.

Pedals without removable dust caps may be oiled from the outside. If lubrication does not make them spin freely, they should be replaced.

Reassemble the cranks on the axle. The tapered pin on the right or chainwheel side should point in the opposite direction from that on the left side. If you failed to note the original position, check to see which end of the pin hole in the crank has the

larger diameter. Start the pin from that end.

Next check the steering head. The fork should turn freely without binding or noise, but there should be no slackness in the bearings. If in doubt, service it. Loosen the handlebar stem bolt about ¼-inch and drive it down with a hammer to free the plug inside the bottom of the stem. Use a block of wood to protect the bolt head. Pull out the bar and stem. Loosen and remove the head locknut, washer and adjusting nut. Hold English bikes over a newspaper for this operation (loose bearings). If the head bearings are in a retainer, typical of German and American made bikes, note which side of the retainer faces upward. The retainer at the bottom of the head will be reversed to that above.

Pull out the fork, and collect all the parts. Clean and grease them. To reassemble, set the bike upside down and put grease in the bottom head cup. Stick the bearings in, and insert the fork with the lower cone on it. Invert the bike, holding the fork tightly in place until the top grease, bearings, and adjusting cone nut are installed. Adjust the cone nut for free movement without end play, and lock it. Replace handlebars.

Inspect the brakes for frayed cables, drag between caliper arms, and thickness

▲ *Use 2x4 block of wood with a ³/₈-inch hole drilled in one end to support crank and accept tapered crank pin as you tap it out. Drill hole close to edge of block.*

➤ *Fork should move freely with no binding or noise. To service it, remove handlebar by backing out stem bolt ¹/₄-inch.*

How to Fix Bicycles

◄ Drive stem bolt down with hammer to free the plug inside the stem. Use a block of wood to protect bolt head.

▼ To service fork bearings, loosen and remove the head, lock nut, washer and adjusting nut. Note position of bearing retainers on German and American bikes. On English bikes, catch loose ball bearings.

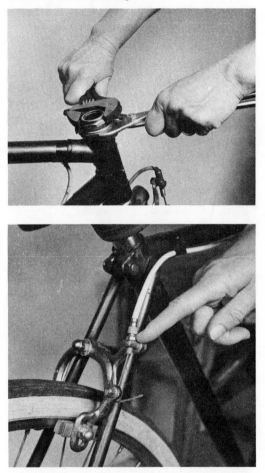

of pads. Replace cables and pads if necessary. Rusty brakes should be removed and scoured with steel wool or a wire brush to remove the corrosion. File off any bumps which restrict movement. When installed, adjust them for about ⅛-inch clearance between pads and the wheel rims. Test for slackness in lever action. Adjustment is made by loosening the locknut from its place against the ledge on a caliper arm and twisting the barrel (see photo). If the barrel adjustment does not take up the slack, loosen the anchor pin and draw more cable through it. Finally, check the pads for correct vertical placement to see that they engage the rim and not the tire.

The saddle height must be properly set to your leg length for efficient pedaling. With the pedal at the bottom position your leg should be slightly bent. The handlebar should be lowered so that you must lean forward a bit, even with a flat bar to reach the grips.

When you have finished the overhaul, don't forget to use the proper pressure in your tires. Low pressure is hard on the tires and on you. About 45 to 50 pounds is right for 26 x 1⅜-inch tires, the most popular size.

New bikes are great, but an old bike

▲ To adjust brakes, loosen lock nut (under finger) and twist knurled barrel (above finger) until brake pad clears rim by ⅛-inch. For further adjustment, loosen anchor pin and pull cable through.

gives you two-way fun—rebuilding as well as riding. Now take off for a ride and see what a difference your work has made. D.W.

How to Buy Binoculars

Good binoculars are a serious investment for any outdoorsman. Learning what to look for can mean the difference between a good buy and money thrown to the wind

THE ONLY WAY a camper, hunter or inland angler can convert a big valley into a small one is to use binoculars, which magically whisk one's sight over the vale for a closeup look at the other side.

Good glasses can be highly useful to the outdoorsman, whether purchased new, or second-hand, maybe in a swap. The important word is "good," for bad glasses are an abomination.

Yet there can be a difference of perhaps $20 between binoculars that to a casual eye seem virtually identical. Naturally you'd want the less expensive pair. Sometimes they can be as good as the more costly glasses. Sometimes not, and you're better off paying extra.

How do you tell the difference?

First, by understanding binocular basics, which aren't especially difficult to absorb. And then by making a series of checks of the binoculars you think you may purchase. Let's view basics first:

Binoculars are identified by two numbers, for example: 7x35. The first number is the power. The image is increased in apparent size that many times. The second number is the diameter of the front lens, which is called the objective lens.

If you hold the glasses up, well away from the eye, and look through them you'll see a small dot of light. This is the exit pupil, and its diameter can be useful knowledge when buying old binoculars from which lettering may have worn off. The exit pupil diameter can be measured, with a millimeter rule and great care.

Divide exit pupil diameter into objective lens diameter and you have the power. Example: a 5-mm exit pupil divided into a 35-mm objective gives you seven-power. The glasses are 7x35's. Conversely, dividing the stated power into the measured objective lens diameter *should give you the exact pupil diameter*. If you know any two for certain, you can determine the third.

The objective lens really provides the light-gathering power: 7x50's have an objective lens larger than 7x35's, so admit more light. Often you'll hear people assert that it is exit pupil diameter which determines light-gathering power, but the exit pupil is really the objective lens, reduced to a dot in apparent size, as it is viewed

How to Buy Binoculars

through the length of the optical system. The bigger the objective lens, in relation to the power, the bigger the exit pupil.

You can use exit pupil diameter to estimate relative brightness. Square it, and if the lenses are *fully* coated (more about that later) add 50 per cent. A 5-mm exit pupil, squared, is 25; plus 50 per cent is 37.5. That's your "relative" brightness. Hence, 6x30's and 7x35's both show 37.5 in relative brightness. But 7x50's are 76.4 in brightness—quite a difference! That's why 7x50's are good "night glasses."

Field of view is merely the width of the field in feet at 1,000 yards. You can't check it without hiking and measuring.

Start examining binoculars by moving all parts, lock to lock—as far as they'll go, in both directions.

This includes the focus, including that for one individual eye as well as center-focus wheels; and the eye-width adjustment—which is known as interpupillary distance. Rack 'em back and forth, in and out, all the way. If you have power zoom binoculars in hand, do the same thing—all the way out, and back.

Check for smoothness of operation, with no end play, no binding, no hang-up. Good, new binoculars should work smoothly. Older, second-hand binoculars may be a bit hard to move. The original grease may have hardened.

Now hold the binoculars up to your ear and *listen* while you repeat the operation with all moving parts. You are checking now for poor machining, and *listening* to binoculars is a good clue to this factor.

If not blocked out by background noise, you may hear a slight crackling sound. This means the worker assembling the binoculars put stiff grease on badly machined and fitted parts to make them operate more smoothly.

You should also look for grease—especially if you think you hear it. It can leak out under the oculars and at fitted sub-assemblies. A sloppy job of assembly means the worker may not even make an attempt to wipe the revealing grease away to conceal what was done.

Now turn the binoculars around end-for-end, hold them fairly close to the eye, and look through them from the objective lens—look through the "wrong" end.

This reveals the inside of the glasses. You should be able to spot scratched, chipped prisms, diecasting imperfections, and fungus—a white, spidery growth.

Hold the glasses down, objective lens somewhat further from the eye, so the objective lenses reflect an overhead light. It should be a fluorescent light, but you can teach yourself, with practice, to use more conventional lamps.

What are you looking for? The quality of the coating on the lenses. Nowadays coating is used to hold down loss of light from reflection, and improve optical efficiency. But it can be badly done, or the label may fib about the degree.

By looking down into the wrong end (objective lens), you can spot where edges of a lens might have been missed—maybe the lens was placed upon its support lopsided for the coating process. You can also spot holes and bare spots.

▲ *Listen while you operate; then focus all the way in and out. A slight crackling sound means heavy grease has been used to mask poor machining of parts.*

The *reflections* of that fluorescent light overhead should be almost the same color, a bluish cast. You'll see more than one reflection because there is more than one lens surface. If both are bluish, your lenses are *fully* coated. But if one is blue, and the other a whitish yellow, then the lenses are only *half-coated*.

All good binoculars are fully coated. Often the manufacturer says so in accompanying literature or in labeling.

Some binoculars, however, claim only to be "coated." And these may turn out to be "half" coated.

The difference in the manufacturing process is about one dollar, so you should go for fully coated optics as a matter of preference, especially if there is a substantial price difference suggesting there were manufacturing shortcuts taken elsewhere.

Dollar here, dollar there—but you can go too far.

Now examine the outside. You are looking for a clean, neat assembly and finishing job, and you don't have to be an expert to spot imperfections here. You also want to know if the binoculars have interpupillary and diopter scales—those markings on the eyewidth and one-eyepiece adjustments. Good binoculars always have them. They make it easy for the owner to instantly readjust the glasses to his own particular sight requirements after someone else has borrowed them for a moment and jiggled everything about to suit himself. You simply learn, from short experience, what scale settings make the glasses just right for you and your eyes.

You may also want to see if the binoculars have retractable eyecups. These are in-out adjustments on the cups themselves, and are very useful to eyeglass wearers. You turn them in when wearing glasses, out when you are not. It can be important. If the glasses aren't the right distance from the eye, you lose part of that all-important field of view.

▲ *Look into wrong end to spot cracked or chipped prisms, imperfections in die casting of parts and fungus (a white, spider-web-like growth).*

➤ *Reflect light, preferably fluorescent, off the objective lens. If the lens is fully coated, both reflections that you see will have a bluish tint. Look for flaws in the coating.*

◄ Grease leaking from fitted assemblies can mean slipshod work on the production line.

▼ Look through binoculars at a brick wall, or other surface with regular horizontal and vertical lines. If verticals and horizontals do not have equal sharpness, don't buy the binoculars.

Last of all, look through the glasses. Adjust one eyepiece, if center focus type; or adjust both, if they are individual focus. Watch very carefully to see if there is any eccentric motion which would indicate that the optical and physical centers are not aligned.

Also look at the color of the image. There may be some slight color fringe, and if it is *slight* the glasses can still be acceptable. But if it is markedly present, the lens system has chromatic aberration. Pass it up. And if there is an overall grayish cast, subduing contrast, you could have other optical aberrations. Focus the glasses on a brick or stone wall, where you have horizontal and vertical lines. Both should focus with equal sharpness. If they do not —if one is sharper then the other—you have spherical aberration. Pass the glasses up.

You can also look for curvature, which is a mild distortion of the image somewhat similar to that produced by a wide-angle camera lens. Some is almost always present, but scarcely noticeable. It arises from the desire to effect useful compromise,

combining the most possible power with the widest field of view. This is a matter of individual taste and tolerance. Sports fans want a lot of power and a wide field, too.

If your binoculars pass all, or nearly all, the tests outlined above you have a serviceable set of glasses. But you should also ask yourself a few more questions to determine their suitability for the precise purpose you have in mind.

Taking power as an example, nearly everyone wants too much of it. There is a limit to the degree of power that can be held in the hand. Some people begin developing visible tremor in the image hand-holding eight-power glasses. More see this detail-destroying action at ten-power, a practical limit for the average person.

There is also the field of view to consider. For some activities you want a wide field (watching football, or use on a lively small boat, are both good examples). With too small a field of view either the action moves easily out of your field (football) or else the bobbing about of your platform makes it impossible to hold the glasses steady on a subject (boating).

Bird watchers, considering another use of glasses, aren't so much interested in a wide field of view. They want the most practical power, usually with compactness and light weight. Campers, hikers and fishermen can use almost any glass of moderate magnification. Hunters care less, perhaps, about a wide field than they do for power—and they often can make use of some steadying test—a boulder, a tree—so as to use even higher power glasses than most of us would want.

So be sure you choose a degree of magnification, coupled with the best field of view, for your purposes. Six-power is plenty for small boat owners. Those 7x50's are great on larger craft operated at night. They even seem to multiply available light, and you can guide a boat past the channel buoys with very little light. But even on large hulls they're hard to use when a sea is running.

Campers, hunters and birdwatchers can go to eight-power glasses. Normally, neither they nor their subjects are bobbing about. Birdwatchers, however (and we all watch birds now and then) should be certain they can focus fairly close. Some glasses just won't focus down to 12 or 15 feet, and often—especially in a woodland camp—birds may wander that close to the site.

Once you buy—or swap for—a pair of binoculars, you should take good care of them. Binoculars are like flowers. They need light and air—*but not too much!* You should never, most particularly in a warm and humid climate, put glasses in their case and then store them in a dark drawer or closet corner. Darkness encourages the growth of fungus on the optical system. Leave them out, if possible, or store them away out of their case, exposed to the air, and to some light.

But do not subject them to excessive heat or direct sunlight. It can melt the balsam used as cement on the lens elements. Even the grease can vaporize, coat the interior, and perhaps the lenses. This has happened in store windows.

Don't injudiciously expose your costly glasses to weather, either. If they've been used in light rain, wipe the body down with a clean cloth. Clean the lenses with the same type of tissue or cloth sold for use on eyeglasses or camera lenses. And don't use an old bandanna or handkerchief! It can cause damage in the form of light scratches.

You'll note that two forms of moisture accumulation periodically occur. Fog forms *inside* the glasses. It arises from sudden conflict in temperature and humidity, and clears up after the glasses sit for awhile, adjusting to the change. Fog shows up when you take the glasses out of a case, perhaps in a warm room or cabin, and step outside into cooler, more moist, air. All you can do is wait.

But condensation is something else. It forms on the outside of the lenses and can be wiped off—although you may have to wipe it more than once to eliminate it.

Last of all, don't take binoculars apart. It isn't difficult, more's the pity; any average American male, cursed with typical mechanical curiosity, may reach for a screwdriver and go to work.

Mechanically, it may not be a problem. But putting binoculars back together again can be. You may never get the optical elements properly in line.

Leave 'em alone. And they'll give you years of service, making big valleys into small ones.   J.M.

See also: CAMPING; HUNTING; NAVIGATION.

▲ The small dot of light seen when you hold binoculars away from eyes and look through them is the exit pupil. Divide its diameter into that of objective lens to figure binocular power.

▲ Before you buy a pair of binoculars, operate all the adjustments all the way in each direction. Make sure the operation is smooth and that there is no jamming or binding.

BINOCULAR PURPOSE CHART

USES	6X,15	6X,30	7X,35	7X,35B.F.*	7X,50	8X,30	8X,40	8.5X,44	10X,50	Zoom
ALL PURPOSE	A	A	A	B	B	B	B	C	D	B
INDOOR SPORTS	A	A	A	B	C	B	C	C	D	A
HORSE RACING	B	A	A	A	A	A	A	A	D	A
OUTDOOR SPORTS	A	A	A	A	B	B	B	B	D	B
YACHTING	B	A	A	A	A	B	B	B	C	B
HUNTING (wooded)	B	A	B	B	B	B	A	B	D	B
HUNTING (semi-wooded)	B	A	B	B	C	A	A	B	D	A
HUNTING (open)	B	B	B	A	B	A	A	B	B	A
HUNTING (mountain)	C	C	A	A	B	A	A	A	A	A
BIRDING	B	A	A	B	B	B	A	A	C	B
HIKING	A	A	A	B	C	B	B	B	D	B
TOURING	A	A	A	B	B	A	A	A	B	A
NIGHT USE	B	B	B	B	A	B	B	B	C	B

LEGEND: (A) Excellent (B) Good (C) Fair (D) Not Recommended
*Broad Field

Provide either a one-or two-course meal for the birds in your area with these feeders that are inexpensive, decorative and functional.

Bird Feeding Stations

Some people spend large sums of money for an aviary; but you can enjoy the same benefits with an inexpensive bird sanctuary

AMATEUR ORNITHOLOGY is a popular hobby. Being able to identify birds by appearance, actions, habits, and song are rewards that a person can enjoy year-round, especially if he has a bird sanctuary in his backyard.

Birds may not flock to your feeding stations at first, but don't be discouraged because it takes time for them to find out about it. Once your station is discovered the birds in your area will come to rely on it, especially during the months when nature is unable to supply them with food. It's during this time of the year that they depend on you for their very existence.

Establishing a bird sanctuary in your

backyard requires a minimum of equipment: one or more feeding stations, a water-filled container for drinking and bathing, and several nesting boxes.

Nesting boxes should be in a sheltered spot for protection against cold, wind, and rain. Books on various types of nesting boxes preferred by certain species that inhabit your vicinity are available at the library.

To speed erection and keep waste to a minimum, lay out the required components for the wall feeder on the ¾-inch surfaced pine (see Materials List) and cut to size. After the pieces are cut, sand with 2/0 garnet paper so the final sanding job will be easier. When assembling the feeder, apply glue to joining members for added strength.

Set your saw blade and make the ⅜ x ¾-inch rabbet cuts at the ends of the bottom member so the sides fit snug when they are attached. Use a scroll or saber saw to cut the shape detail and window openings in the sides. For added strength and protection against the elements, the sides are dadoed so the tempered hardboard back panel can be slipped into place.

Make a 15° bevel on the outside edge of the rear roof rafter so the feeder can fit snug against the wall, then use the same degree setting to rip a ⅛ x ⅜-inch dado that runs parallel to the back edge. This groove acts as a barrier to prevent water from dripping into the feeder. The lower part of the back is nailed to the bottom of the feeder so water can drain off.

Cut the shutters from the ¼-inch exterior plywood and attach them to the sides with ⅜-inch brads. Cross-nail the sides to the bottom with 7*d* common nails

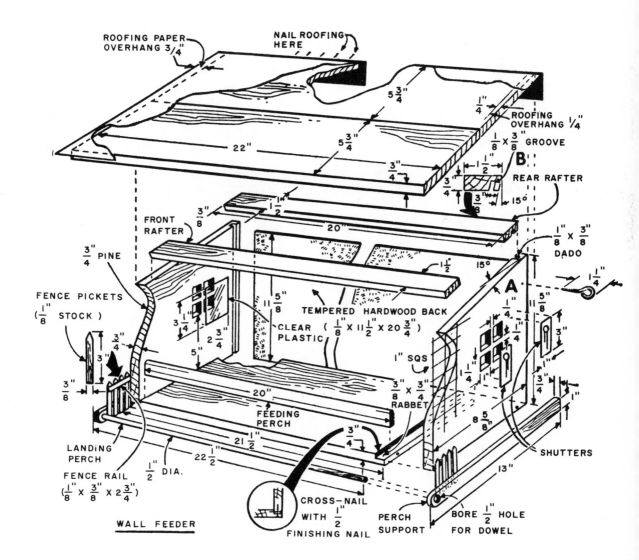

WALL FEEDER

▲ *Attach the rear rafter so the beveled edge fits flush with the back of the side walls and the groove fits snug over the hardboard back.*

▲ *Brad the fence to the inside of the perch support before nailing the supports and perch dowel to the feeder with finishing nails.*

and insert the hardboard back. Use 1½-inch finishing nails to attach the rafters and feeding perch.

Use a file to shape the points on the pickets and attach them to the rail with ⅜-inch brads. After bradding the fencing to the landing perch supports, attach the supports to the feeder with 4d finishing nails.

Before you install the two ¾ x 5¾ x 22-inch roof sections, bevel the front and

MATERIALS LIST—Wall Feeder

Quantity	Size and Description	Purpose
1	³/₄″ 10″x8′ pine	floor, walls, rafters
1	¹/₄″ 22″x23″ exterior plywood	hoppers, shutters
1	⅛″ 11⅝″x20¾″ tempered hardboard	back
1	½″x22½″ dowel	landing perch
1	⅛″ ⅜″x30½″ molding	fence rail, pickets
1	³/₄″ 13″x23½″ red roofing	roof
2	4¼″x4½″ No. 24 gauge galvanized sheet metal	chutes
2	4¼″x6¾″ window pane	hopper fronts
2 each	1¼″ eyes, 2¼″ hooks	
as needed	1½″ common nails	
as needed	1½″ finishing nails	
as needed	1″ lath nails	
as needed	³/₄″ roofing nails	
as needed	³/₄″ brads	
as needed	½″ brads	
as needed	⅜″ brads	

NOTE: Also need, abrasives, glue, paint, and clear plastic.

Bird Feeding Stations

back. After these edges are shaped, use finishing nails to attach the pieces to the sides and rafters.

The seed hopper is designed so you know when to add feed, and can replenish the food supply without undue waste. The seed container, which is made of ¼-inch exterior plywood, has a glass front so you can see when feed must be added. When the supply gets low, take the hopper out, remove the top, and pour in the feed.

Guide strips hold the glass in place and 1¼-inch finishing nails are installed at the bottom to act as seed guards. The seed is fed to the 1-inch opening by a sheet metal chute nailed to the back and bottom of the hopper. After you cut the glass fronts, dull the sharp edges with coarse silicon, carbide abrasive paper, cloth, or oilstone.

If small millet seeds are used as food, space the nails ⅜-inches apart. For wild bird seed mixture, space them at least ⅝-inches apart to prevent large seeds, such as the sunflower, from clogging the openings.

Re-sand the surfaces with 6/0 abrasive paper and apply a coat of green exterior primer. When it dries, rub the surface smooth with medium grade steel wool. Dust thoroughly and finish with two coats of outdoor enamel.

Install the 90-pound red roofing by spacing the nails about 4 inches apart and ½-inch from the front and side edges. Bend the rear overhang down and nail it to the roof. Form drip eaves on the ends and front by bending the roofing down.

Cover the window openings with a clear plastic that you can buy at a stationary store of lumber yard. Coat the edges with adhesive and nail on the inside with ½-inch brads.

Attach the feeder to the wall with the hooks and eyes. Keep it at least 7 feet above the ground to prevent cats and other enemies from preying on the feeding birds. The protruding perch prevents cats from getting into the feeder because they cannot

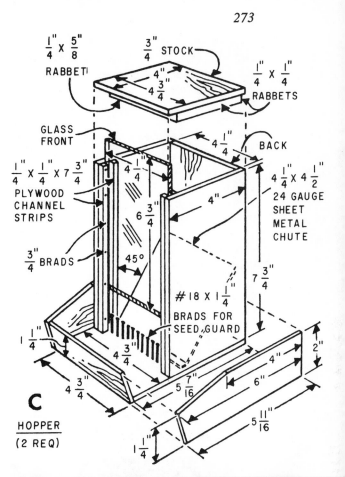

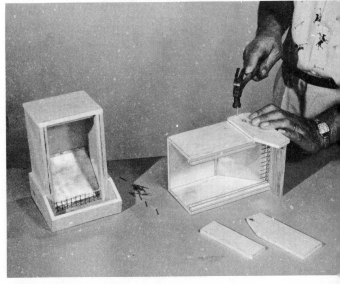

▲ *Each hopper holds 2 lbs. of seed. Metal chutes direct the feed toward the seed guards.*

get a foothold for their rear feet. Birds will continue to visit the feeder as long as they are sure that no danger exists.

The circular feeder can be hung from a roof eave or suspended from a crossarm attached to a post or other support.

Let the lady of the house participate in building it by supplying you with the kitchen utensils that are used (see Materials List), such as the cake and pie tins and a quart-size canning jar that has an open type screw cap. If she doesn't have a ⅜ x 13-inch pizza tin, you can buy one at a variety store, or cut the roof disk from sheet metal.

Start this project by cutting two ⅜ x 6¾-inch strips from a piece of No. 24 gauge galvanized sheet metal. Bend these strips over the rim of the 6-inch pie tin and solder. Use a compass to mark an opening on the 9-inch cake tin that is large enough to accept the pie tin. Drill a starter hole and use a saber saw equipped with a metal cutting blade to cut the circular opening.

Drill eight holes in the rim of the cake tin for the perch ring support rods and chain links. You can use coat hanger wire or welding rods for the supports. Cut into 4-inch lengths and flatten one end so the rods can be riveted and soldered to the side of the cake tin. Use pliers to shape the rod before you attach it.

The bending jig can be used to shape the ¼-inch copper tubing into a ring for the perch. Once the circle is formed, insert the ends in a metal coupler and crimp with a metal punch. Solder the connection for added strength.

Position the support rods on the 15-inch diameter circle and drill ⅛-inch holes through one side of the copper tubing for the supports. Fit the rods into the holes and solder to the tubing.

Assemble the cupola by joining two ¾ x 3¾-inch disks with finishing nails and attach a 4½-inch plywood cap with brads. Use a ½-inch drill bit to bore the eight holes in the cupola. Center the cupola on the indented side of the pizza tin and

MATERIALS LIST—Circular Feeder		
Quantity	**Size and Description**	**Purpose**
1	1″x9″ cake tin	seed tray
1	1″x6″ pie tin	seed tray
1	⅜″x13″ pizza tin	roof
1	3¾″x7⅛″ canning jar	seed dispenser
2	¾″x3¾″ pine	cupola
1	¼″x4¼″ exterior plywood	cupola cap
1	¼″x48″ copper tubing	perch ring
1	9/64″x¾″ metal rod	perch ring coupler
4	⅛″x4″ metal rods	ring supports
4	¼″ #18 escutcheon pins	rivets
1	¾″x10″ No. 24 gauge galvanized sheet metal	jar support strips and clips
1	5/16″x64″ jack chain	connectors
1	½″x1¼″ china link	feed coupler
8	1″ lath nails	cupola
NOTE: Also need, solder, finishing nails, brads and metal primer.		

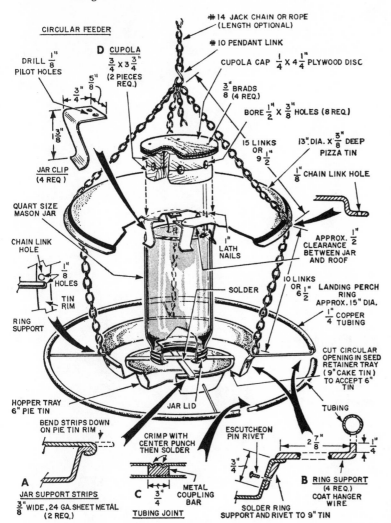

CIRCULAR FEEDER

DRILL $\frac{1}{8}$"
PILOT HOLES

D CUPOLA
$\frac{3}{4}$" X 3 $\frac{3}{4}$"
(2 PIECES REQ.)

$\frac{3}{4}$" $\frac{5}{8}$"

1 $\frac{3}{8}$"

JAR CLIP
(4 REQ)

#14 JACK CHAIN OR ROPE
(LENGTH OPTIONAL)

#10 PENDANT LINK

CUPOLA CAP $\frac{1}{4}$" X 4 $\frac{1}{4}$" PLYWOOD DISC

$\frac{3}{8}$" BRADS
(4 REQ.)

BORE $\frac{1}{2}$" X $\frac{3}{8}$" HOLES (8 REQ.)

15 LINKS OR 9 $\frac{1}{2}$"

13" DIA. X $\frac{5}{8}$" DEEP PIZZA TIN

$\frac{1}{8}$" CHAIN LINK HOLE

QUART SIZE MASON JAR

CHAIN LINK HOLE

$\frac{1}{8}$" HOLES

TIN RIM

RING SUPPORT

LATH NAILS

APPROX. $\frac{1}{2}$" CLEARANCE BETWEEN JAR AND ROOF

SOLDER

10 LINKS OR 6 $\frac{1}{2}$"   LANDING PERCH RING APPROX. 15" DIA.

$\frac{1}{4}$" COPPER TUBING

HOPPER TRAY
6" PIE TIN

BEND STRIPS DOWN ON PIE TIN RIM

A

JAR SUPPORT STRIPS
$\frac{3}{8}$" WIDE, 24 GA. SHEET METAL
(2 REQ.)

CRIMP WITH CENTER PUNCH THEN SOLDER

C $\frac{3}{4}$"

METAL COUPLING BAR

TUBING JOINT

JAR LID

ESCUTCHEON PIN RIVET

$\frac{3}{4}$"

CUT CIRCULAR OPENING IN SEED RETAINER TRAY (9" CAKE TIN) TO ACCEPT 6" TIN

TUBING

2 $\frac{7}{8}$"   1 $\frac{1}{4}$"

B RING SUPPORT
(4 REQ.)
COAT HANGER WIRE

SOLDER RING SUPPORT AND RIVET TO 9" TIN

▲ *Attach the support rods that lead from the cake tin to the perch by drilling four holes and soldering the coat hanger wire to the ring.*

▼ *Shape the ring for the landing perch by bending the copper tubing around a board that has a 7-in.-radius curve bandsawed on one side.*

mark the circumference with a pencil or scoring awl. Use this circle as a guide when nailing the jar clips. Drill pilot holes through the clips and roof so you can drive the 1-inch lath nails into the cupola without bending.

Coat all parts with a metal primer. The best way to paint the chain is to immerse it in a mixture of equal parts of paint and thinner and hang it on a nail to dry. Cut the chain into four 16-inch lengths and connect the cake tin and perch unit to the roof so the bottom of the feed jar is ½-inch from the roof.

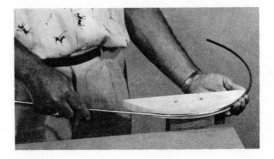

By leaving the bottom loop open on one of the connecting chains where it attaches to the cake tin, the jar can be taken out for replenishing the food supply.   F.H.

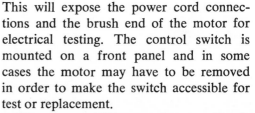

Repair Your Blender

If your blender doesn't work, use these techniques to spot the part to be replaced

THE BLENDER is a two-part appliance comprising a base or power unit and a blending container. All the work is done in the glass blending container.

Aside from cracking or breaking this glass container, the only things that can go wrong are damaged cutting blades or a leaky seal. These parts can be replaced easily if they don't function properly.

The base power unit contains the motor and electrical speed control switch.

The motor used is a series or universal type because it will deliver the high speed needed for complete blending or liquidizing of the material placed in the container. Operating speeds may be as high as 16,000 rpm.

Most blender power units are accessible for service by removing the base plate.

This will expose the power cord connections and the brush end of the motor for electrical testing. The control switch is mounted on a front panel and in some cases the motor may have to be removed in order to make the switch accessible for test or replacement.

The greatest difference between blenders is in the method of motor speed control. They may have rotary switches, toggle switches or push button switches, each requiring a different electrical circuit.

Electrical testing is done with a volt-ohmmeter. This device is used to determine if voltage is available to the motor. The ohmmeter portion will indicate the condition of the switch and the electrical windings of the motor.

Before making any electrical tests, try

Repair Your Blender

to turn the motor by hand, using your fingers to turn the drive lug. If it doesn't turn, the armature is frozen. Clean the motor bearings and lubricate them. If this doesn't solve the problem, continue trouble-shooting.

When using the volt meter section of the volt-ohmmeter, the blender must be plugged into a wall socket. The meter switch should be set at the 150-volt AC position.

During the tests a line voltage of about 115 volts should be obtained when the leads are connected to: (1) the wall socket —no voltage indicates a defective socket; (2) the connection of the power cord to the switch and motor—no voltage indicates a defective cord; (3) the motor connection of the power cord and the other side of the switch, with the switch turned on—no voltage indicates a defective switch.

If voltage is available up to the motor and the motor does not operate, it is probably defective.

Each electrical part can be tested individually with the ohmmeter. Follow the instructions with the meter to change over resistance readings. Turn the switch of the meter to the R x 1 position. *Caution:* unplug the cord from the wall outlet before making these continuity tests.

The line cord should show continuity (zero ohms) from each terminal on its plug to the end of its wire. The switch should show continuity from terminal to terminal when it is on and no continuity (infinity, shown by a sideways figure 8 on the dial) when it is off. The motor should show a resistance reading. No continuity would indicate it to be burned out. Any defective part should be replaced. Switches and motors of blenders are not ordinarily repairable.

The most commonly used tools are either a standard or Phillips screwdriver. A nut driver may be needed in some models to remove the switch or disassemble the motor.

Although defective parts will have to be replaced, an exception could be a loose or broken wire or a power cord that is broken at the plug end or at the point where it is clamped under the strain relief. The loose or broken wire can be resoldered

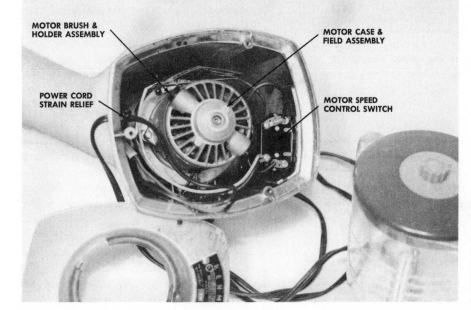

MOTOR BRUSH & HOLDER ASSEMBLY

MOTOR CASE & FIELD ASSEMBLY

POWER CORD STRAIN RELIEF

MOTOR SPEED CONTROL SWITCH

◀*Blender base power unit with bottom cover removed. Brushes can be examined by removing the caps from the brush holder. When replacing brushes, make certain curved end contacts armature commutator in exactly the same way as before it was removed.*

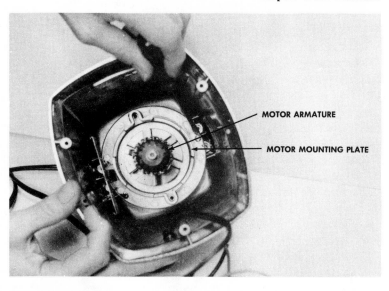

MOTOR ARMATURE

MOTOR MOUNTING PLATE

➤ *Motor armature is accessible after field coil and motor housing have been removed.*

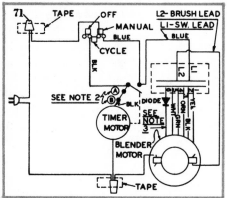

⬆ *Several taps in the field winding and a diode inserted in the circuit provide 10 different speeds in this blender circuit.*

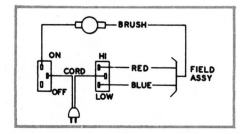

⬆ *This simple two-speed circuit derives its speed change from a tap in the field winding.*

and the power cord can be shortened and reconnected.

Parts should be available from a dealer who handles the particular make you have. If the dealer does not have the parts or says that he can not get them, try the manufacturer of the blender. Sources are usually listed in the yellow pages of your telephone book under "Electric Appliances—Small—Repairing." There are very few mail order parts outlets that might have all the special parts for the many different blenders in use. There are some very good small motor repair specialists who could repair or replace defective motors or any parts. These specialists are usually located in a major metropolitan area, listed in the yellow pages under "Electric Motors—Dealers & Repairing."

When reassembling the unit make certain some good light grade of oil is applied sparingly to the shaft and bearing. Be sure the armature turns freely by hand before applying power.

A word of caution—before getting too involved in a major repair, consider the cost of a new blender. Also consider the age of the unit requiring service and the potential cost of parts. Motors, armatures

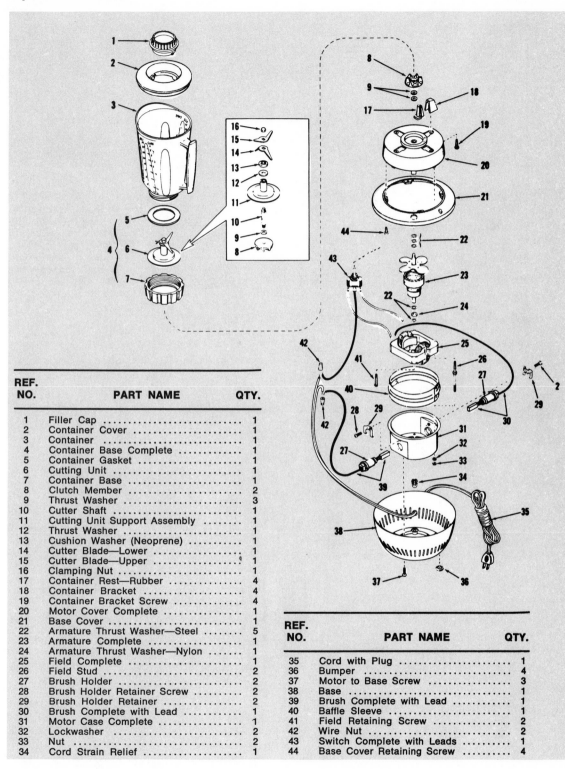

REF. NO.	PART NAME	QTY.
1	Filler Cap	1
2	Container Cover	1
3	Container	1
4	Container Base Complete	1
5	Container Gasket	1
6	Cutting Unit	1
7	Container Base	1
8	Clutch Member	2
9	Thrust Washer	3
10	Cutter Shaft	1
11	Cutting Unit Support Assembly	1
12	Thrust Washer	1
13	Cushion Washer (Neoprene)	1
14	Cutter Blade—Lower	1
15	Cutter Blade—Upper	1
16	Clamping Nut	1
17	Container Rest—Rubber	4
18	Container Bracket	4
19	Container Bracket Screw	4
20	Motor Cover Complete	1
21	Base Cover	1
22	Armature Thrust Washer—Steel	5
23	Armature Complete	1
24	Armature Thrust Washer—Nylon	1
25	Field Complete	1
26	Field Stud	2
27	Brush Holder	2
28	Brush Holder Retainer Screw	2
29	Brush Holder Retainer	2
30	Brush Complete with Lead	1
31	Motor Case Complete	1
32	Lockwasher	2
33	Nut	2
34	Cord Strain Relief	1

REF. NO.	PART NAME	QTY.
35	Cord with Plug	1
36	Bumper	4
37	Motor to Base Screw	3
38	Base	1
39	Brush Complete with Lead	1
40	Baffle Sleeve	1
41	Field Retaining Screw	2
42	Wire Nut	2
43	Switch Complete with Leads	1
44	Base Cover Retaining Screw	4

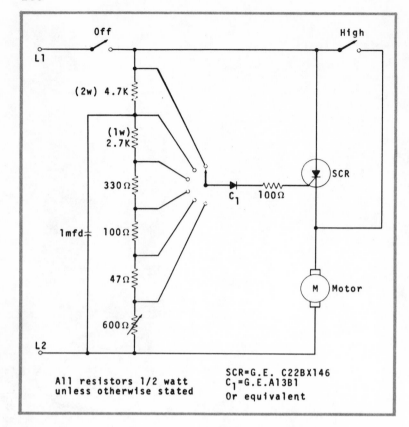

In this wiring diagram, the silicon controlled rectifier (SCR) controls the voltage available to the motor, reducing speed by about 2000 RPM per switch step.

BLENDER TROUBLE CHART

PROBLEM	POSSIBLE CAUSE										
	NO POWER	DEFECTIVE CORD	DEFECTIVE SWITCH	DEFECTIVE MOTOR	BAD BEARINGS	INCORRECT CONTAINER PLACEMENT	DEFECTIVE COUPLING	CRACKED CONTAINER	LEAKY SEAL	BENT BLADES	(LOOSE)
MOTOR WON'T RUN	√	√	√	√	√						
BLADES DON'T TURN						√	√			√	
HIGH SPEED ONLY			√								
LOW SPEED ONLY			√	√	√						
LEAKY CONTAINER								√	√		
ABNORMAL NOISE					√					√	√

and multiple contact push button switches are not cheap.

The accompanying check list should serve as a guide in locating a problem.

The accompanying exploded view will serve as a diagram for locating parts.

G.M.

See also: APPLIANCE REPAIR; ELECTRONICS.

Plywood and Lumber

Selecting the right wood
for a boat can be confusing.
Here's what to
look for — and avoid

THE TREMENDOUS upsurge in the popularity of small boats has been fostered by the advent of a reliable marine plywood in long lengths. A plywood boat is light and waterproof. It is strong, and has relatively few seams. Plywood is tough and seldom cracks, but is flexible enough to absorb the shock of rough water. Sheet plywood has stimulated boat building by the amateur. With this material, he is able to build a boat that has all the foregoing desirable characteristics and yet is relatively simple in construction.

The standard plywood available is an engineered wood board or panel. It consists of an odd number of veneer sheets placed crosswise and bonded together under hydraulic pressure with waterproof adhesives, each stronger than the wood itself. The odd number of veneer sheets are used to give a balanced, symmetrical panel construction. This minimizes warping, cupping and twisting. The better veneers are used on the faces of the panels, while lower grade stock is placed in the cores and crossbands. Currently available marine panels have choice veneers for all cores and crossbands. The cross-laminations in plywood minimize the properties in each direction and eliminate almost completely, if not entirely, certain inherent weaknesses of normal lumber. Shrinkage, for example,

boat building materials: see lumber

is reduced in plywood to the point that it is negligible in many services. Splitting is impossible in any direction. Bending strength and stiffness is reduced somewhat lengthwise, but generally increased crosswise, the amount varying, depending on the number and thickness of the plies. The greater number of plies, the greater the utilization of strength in the two directions.

The most commonly used type of plywood is made from Douglas fir. This material comes from the Pacific Northwest and is available in a number of grades. Only exterior grade plywood should be considered for marine construction and boat building. Interior plywood cannot be used, regardless of fiberglass or other coverings. The exterior type can be identified in the United States by the industry's grade trade mark, EXT.-D.F.P.A. This stamp is burned on the edge of the panel and will assure the builder of genuine exterior plywood. There are a wide range of plywoods made from hardwoods or tropical lumber. The most commonly used panels are those manufactured from Philippine mahogany. Many of the hardwood panels have a very thin veneer face. This is objectionable due to the fact that sanding may cut through the top veneer. The strength of such a panel is not good, due to the varying thickness of plies. The cost of mahogany-type plywood is generally considerably higher than Douglas fir plywood. For this reason, mahogany-faced panels are generally relegated to trim, decking, and interior finish.

Currently popular is a fir plywood with a resin-impregnated fiber bonded to the surfaces. This provides additional smoothness and weather-resistance. Such overlays are available in varying densities. The harder types are high-density, and very slick and hard-surfaced. They are not recommended for boat construction, where the panels are subjected to bending. All of these types of panels are stiffer than the conventional panel, and will not take bends as readily. The material is ideal for decks, cabin floors, etc. Many individuals do use the overlaid plywood for planking material. One of the inherent disadvantages is not only the stiffness and resistance to bending, but the difficulty in plugging the fastening areas. After filling the screw cavity with putty, care must be taken in sanding to prevent going through the overlaid surface.

The popularity of Douglas fir plywood has been increased by availability of the material in long panels. The standard size is 48 inches wide and 96 inches long. Thicknesses may vary from ⅛-inch to 1⅛-inch. In some instances, panels 24, 30, and 60 inches wide are stock items. As a rule, panels in length to 20 feet are considered standard. Large sheets can be formed on special order to almost any practical length in 4-foot widths. In most instances, lengths longer than 12 feet are made by splicing shorter panels. The joining is done by a scarf joint to a ratio of 1:12. If the panel is ¼-inch in thickness, the length of the scarf joint would be a minimum of 3 inches. If long length panels are not available in your area, such a scarf joint can be made by the amateur. Considerable care must be taken and the controlling of the glue bond must be carefully done. Except for areas where full length panels are not available, such scarf jointing by the amateur is not recommended. The other method of utilizing short panels when longer ones are not available is by making a simple butt joint.

Douglas fir plywood panels are available in a number of grades. In the exterior or marine type, they are classified as having "A," "B," and "C" faces. Various combinations are available with an "A" veneer on one face, and a "B" or "C" on the other face. For planking panels, "A" faces on both sides are considered best. This is designated by the symbol "A-A." "A-B" grade can be substituted in some in-

▲ *Select plywood for boat building with caution. Use marine or exterior grade plywood, never interior grade.*

stances, and would be ideal for bulkheads, transoms, laminated stems, etc. In places where one side would not be seen, such as on floorboards, cabinets, berth tops, etc., an "A-C" grade can be used. "A"-faced panels will have patches, unfortunately. These will be varying in shape to a maximum of 1 inch, and by D.F.P.A. specifications are edge-glued. Longitudinal chipped areas or strips may also be filled. Considerable care should be taken prior to the purchase of the panel to inspect it carefully. Any of these patches or defects appearing on a panel under stress may tend

to fracture. The "B" veneer panel may have round patches two inches in diameter and are not edge-glued. Such patches, when sprung about the contour of a boat, may tend to pop out. A "C" panel may have knots and open pitch pockets, and therefore is not considered to be practical for planking.

The exterior grade panels are acceptable for plywood boat construction. The disadvantage is that the inner core may have "C" grade veneer panels. These unseen areas, when subjected to bending forces, may cause the panel to fracture. It is also extremely disadvantageous in driving screws to hit a void pocket. Currently available is the premium grade of fir ply-

WEIGHTS OF FIR PLYWOOD	
Thickness	Weights/lbs. Per Square Foot
1/8″	.49
3/16″	.64
1/4″	.80
5/16″	.95
3/8″	1.13
1/2″	1.53
5/8″	1.83
3/4″	2.23
1″	3.00
1 1/8″	3.35

wood specifically intended for boat hull planking. This material, called Marine Exterior, uses the same glue as the exterior panel. The difference is that the specifications for the Marine Exterior calls for virtually solid inner ply construction. This eliminates the core voids that are common in regular exterior plywood. For a boat of any size, the full marine exterior with "A-A" panels is highly recommended.

Plywood planking for covering cannot be used on all boat contours. In fact, the development for plywood planking is quite a complicated process. The sections of a plywood boat will be convex, or in some instances, straight lines. Concave surfaces are not possible. Probably the easiest method of understanding how sheet plywood is used on a boat is to compare it to a piece of paper. Any shape that you can normally bend this sheet of paper without crinkling can be accomplished with the plywood. This is, of course, not taking into consideration the maximum bends that are possible with the wood panel. The surface for plywood planking is developed from segments of a cylinder or a cone. In the latter case, for want of a better term, "con-endric development" is frequently used. Compound surfaces can be obtained with plywood by cutting the panels into strips.

This text is intended to deal primarily with sheet plywood construction.

In any plywood boat, it must be considered that when a panel is bent in a convex shape, the outer surfaces of the panel are in tension, while the inner surfaces are in compression. With excessive bends, the planking may be extremely difficult to apply, and, in some cases, may fracture. Double thicknesses of thinner plywood are then often used. Practical experience is the best teacher for the maximum amount that a plywood panel can be bent. The designer of the particular boat undoubtedly has this experience, and has used it in the particular design that you intend to follow. For practical purposes, on a flat sheet, certain maximum radii to which fir plywood may be bent is available. (See list.)

Many individuals desire information on the weights of Douglas fir plywood. See the list for a rough approximation of these weights.

Lumber. It is impossible to cover all of the types of lumber that are available for boat construction. Each section of the country has certain woods that will be common to that area. As such, they will be less expensive and more readily available. The builder can usually feel safe in substituting lumber for that which is specified, providing it is of the same relative weight and has similar qualities. Attempting to use soft, punky woods for structural members is, naturally, not advocated.

For all members requiring bending, a defect-free, straight-grained stock is used. For framework members, lumber contain-

MAXIMUM BENDS OF FIR PLYWOOD		
Thickness	Radius/lengthwise	Radius/crosswise
1/4″	24″	15″
3/8″	54″	36″
1/2″	8′	6′
5/8″	10′	8′
3/4″	12′	10′

ing minor defects can be tolerated and will generally be cut out. At one time, air-dried stock was the only wood for boat building. With production as it is today, this process has been speeded up, and most lumber available is kiln-dried. Quite often, the moisture content is drier than is advocated for boat building. Moisture content is preferably between 12 and 15%. Lumbers that are dried out to a lesser content can cause serious problems in plywood boat construction. They absorb moisture when put into the water, and can crack seams. If too wet, the wood often checks or cracks after assembly. Over-dried lumber is often brittle and breaks easily.

Lumber is sold by the board foot. A board foot being a measure of size designated as a one-inch thick piece of lumber 12 inches square in the rough (before milling to size). Almost all hardwoods are sold as random-random material in the rough. Random-random means varying widths and lengths. Lumber thicknesses are designated in quarters. Each "quarter" being one-quarter of an inch. Thus, "four-quarters" material is a minimum of one inch in thickness in its rough state. Five-quarters material would be 1¼-inch in rough thickness. When lumber is planed smooth, it will usually lose a minimum of ⅛-inch in thickness. Standard four-quarters material is finished ¾-inch to ¹³⁄₁₆-inch in thickness. Lumber finished in this manner carries the designation S2S, meaning surfaced two sides. In cases where the completely milled S4S (surfaced four sides) lumber is available, approximately ¼-inch is lost in edge finishing. This will mean that the common 1 x 6-inch that would be purchased completely finished, would actually be around ¾ x 5¾-inch.

Considerable savings will be realized if stock is purchased as random-random and ripped to size. If given a choice on the widths of random stock, select the widest possible. This particularly holds true for frame stock. The wider material can be used for nesting several members in one width resulting in less scrap and a lower material cost. Obviously, the builder will have to group his material listings to take advantage of the random material that may be available.

The following list of types of lumber and brief description of each designates some of the more common varieties available in the United States. Also given are the weights of the particular lumber by the cubic foot, and also by the board foot. Obviously, these weights will vary, depending upon the moisture content.

White oak. Weights, 47 pounds per cubic foot; 3.9 pounds per board foot. White oak is a domestic wood grown in the South Atlantic and Central States. White oak is a strong hard wood that holds fastenings very well. It is hard to work, and tools must be kept sharp. Good oak is often hard to obtain in the Far West. The use of oak for all longitudinal members and framework is excellent practice. This lumber has a high concentration of gallic acid. The urea resin type glue should not be used for gluing oak to be submerged in salt water due to the possibility of reaction with the acid.

Red oak. Weights, 44 pounds per cubic foot; 3.7 pounds per board foot. Red oak is grayish-brown in color, usually with a fleshy tinge. A domestic lumber coming from the Southern States, this lumber rots rather easily when in a damp area. For this reason, red oak is generally relegated to interior trim, and is not recommended for framework or longitudinal members.

Philippine mahogany. Weights, 39 pounds per cubic foot; 3.0 pounds per board foot, varies in color from yellowish-brown to reddish-brown. Usually classed as dark red or light red mahogany. The light red is extremely soft, and is usually undesirable except for interior trim. Grown in the Philippine Islands, this material is not a true mahogany, but is a tropical cedar. The dark red variety is probably the most used boat building material being readily worked. It holds fastenings well, and is relatively light in weight. It is used extensively for natural finishing at any place that a rich, natural wood is desired. Glues readily with hardsetting glue, and is reasonable in price.

Honduras mahogany. Weights, 47 pounds per cubic foot; 3.9 pounds per board foot. A deeper red in color and heavier than the Philippine group. Grown in South America, it is a hard, dense wood with less open grain than Philippine. It is used extensively for trim work on the finer boats because of its beautiful grain. It can be used in structures the same as the Philippine, but it is rather expensive.

Douglas fir. Weights, 34 pounds per cubic foot; 2.8 pounds per board foot. Yellow to orange-red in color, Douglas fir is a domestic wood grown in the Northwestern part of the United States. It is a hard wood, but does not bend too readily, and tends to split easily. The vertical grain type can be used in structural assembly, such as framework, longitudinals, etc. The slash grain variety is of little value in boat-building, except for heavy skegs, motor stringer, or similar applications.

Sitka spruce. Weights, 28 pounds per cubic foot; 2.33 pounds per board foot. A very light reddish-brown in color. Sitka spruce grows in the Northwestern coast of North America, from California to Alaska. The wood has a comparatively fine, uniform texture, generally straight-grained. It has moderate light weight, softness, resistance to shock, and small shrinkage. Spruce is frequently used in racing hulls for all members and also for spars on sailing craft. It is easily worked, but difficult to obtain in some areas. For the smaller boat, it is excellent for all structural members. As a weight saver with good strength, it has no peer.

White pine. Weights, 27 pounds per cubic foot; 2.25 pounds per board foot. Cream colored to light reddish-brown in color. It is a domestic wood grown and obtained from the Pacific Northwest. The wood is straight-grained, easily worked, and stays in place after seasoning. The wood is moderately light in weight, but is also moderately low in strength. It is very easily worked, and can be used for interior cabinetry to save weight. It is seldom applicable to structural members.

Port Orford cedar. Weights, 29 pounds per cubic foot; 2.44 pounds per board foot. This lumber is light yellow to pale brown in color, and has a pleasant, spicy odor. It grows along the Pacific Coast from Coos Bay, Oregon, southward to California. It is a moderately strong, clear, and straight-grained material that is popularly used for planking on small boats. Can be used for framing and longitudinal members. The heart wood is extremely resistant to decay and shrinks moderately, with little tendency to warp.

Cypress (bald). Weights, 32 pounds per cubic foot; 2.67 pounds per board foot. Cypress ranges in color from a light yellow-brown to reddish-brown. A domestic wood that comes primarily from the Southern States. Cypress is used for almost every part of a boat where great strength is not required. It is therefore seldom used on structural framework. It is soft and takes a fine finish but has poor fastening holding power.

Longleaf yellow pine. Weights, 41 pounds per cubic foot; 3.42 pounds per board foot. A domestic lumber that comes from the South Atlantic States, orange to reddish-brown in color. Longleaf yellow pine is a strong, very durable, straight-grained material. It is often used as a substitute for white oak for keels and structural longitudinals, as well as framework.

G.L.W.

See also: ADHESIVES; BOAT BUILDING PROJECTS; BOATING; MAINTENANCE, BOAT; WOOD BENDING.

How to Build Plywood Boats

A guide for the beginning boat builder — these basic techniques are used by the pros

FIBERGLASS may be the number one choice for production-line boats, but when it comes to the amateur, plywood remains the overwhelming favorite.

And well it should be. It's cheap, strong, easy to handle, and it provides a handsome boat—whether outboard skiff or an ocean-cruising sailboat.

Although only average carpentry skill is needed, building a boat is not much like building a kitchen corner cabinet. Here are standard procedures that apply to all plywood boat construction, whether you are starting with a set of plans, or building from a kit with pre-cut parts.

First, a word about materials is in order. Of course, the plywood must be marine or exterior grade. Any other type will deteriorate rapidly when exposed to a marine environment. In addition to the plywood itself, everything else that goes into or onto the boat must be suitable for a marine environment. This includes adhesives, fastenings, and paint. Your local marine dealer is the best source for each of these. Do *not* use common brass fastenings in the hull, if it will be kept in salt water. If such fastenings trap moisture, they corrode rapidly.

Plans and patterns. Measurements for many framing members can be taken from the plans and marked directly on the wood stock. Where curves must be cut, full size patterns should be used. The heavy paper available from building supply firms is excellent for patterns.

Plans usually show a scaled-down "pattern" for each curved member, with grid superimposed over it. The grid may represent one- or two-inch squares. Mark off full-size squares on the paper, and draw in the outline for each item, using the plans as your guide.

To transfer the pattern to the stock, tape the pattern in place, and tap a nail through the drawing at two- or three-inch intervals to leave a line of indentations in the wood. Remove the pattern, connect the indentations with a heavy pencil line, and you're ready to cut. Naturally, you cut a little outside of the line, and use a plane or rasp to achieve the finished shape.

Building forms or jigs. For most boats, it's necessary to set up a building form or jig (two words for the same thing) to support frames, transom, and stem during construction. The jig ensures that frames are at the proper intervals, and at right angles to—and centered on—the keel's centerline. It is also used to set up the frames at the proper height in relation to each other.

Often, the plans will give complete instructions for building the form. Because each type of boat has its own requirements, no special instructions can be given here, other than to make sure it is set up to do its job properly, and that it rests on a firm foundation that will not shift or settle during construction.

Keels, stems, transom, knees. These members make up a boat's backbone. Use the best grade wood you can get—wood that is clear, uniform in grain, and free of knots. While solid timbers may be called for in your plans, it is possible to laminate several layers of thin wood to achieve the required thickness, and wind up with a stronger unit than solid wood would provide.

Transom knees and stem are often made up in sections that fit together like pieces of a jigsaw puzzle, with glue and bolts at the joints. Sometimes it is desirable to add plywood side pieces (gussets).

Transoms and frames. These are the first units to be mounted on the building jig in most cases. As they determine the final shape of the boat, every care must be taken to ensure accuracy in their construction.

The transom itself is usually heavy plywood, ¾-inch thick, backed on the inside with ¾-inch framing members. The total 1½-inch thickness along all stress areas provides plenty of strength for outboard motor installations.

To make up the transom, cut the plywood to shape, allowing a little excess for trimming. Cut the framing members to shape and size, and fasten them to the plywood. Coat mating surfaces with waterproof glue, and insert screws *through* the plywood *into* the framing members. Always drill pilot holes for the screws, and countersink the heads.

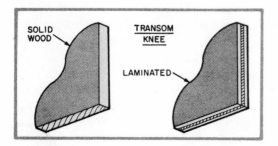

▲ Transom knees are used at the center of the transom. Laminated knees made of plywood have good strength in all directions.

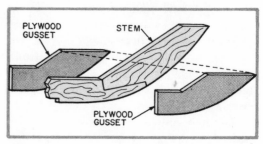

▲ Two-piece stem with gussets. Other methods of construction include laminated plywood (this is the easiest method) or lumber.

How to Build Plywood Boats

Note: Framing members should be notched to take keel, chines, sheer clamps, and stringers or battens as required. Cut the notches before fastening the framing to the plywood.

Frames are usually made up with corner gussets, or with overlap joints at the corners. Both methods are good, and your plans will indicate the correct one for your boat.

Notch frames to take keel, chines, sheer clamps, and battens or stringers, as required. After the keel and bottom stringers are fastened in place, you can make the cuts that provide limber holes. (These allow water to drain past frames.)

Set up the transom, frames, and stem member on the building form. Be sure they are properly aligned and centered; take your time and check carefully before clamping or fastening them to the form.

Longitudinals. These are the keel, chines, sheer clamps, and any stringers or battens that your plans may show. In most

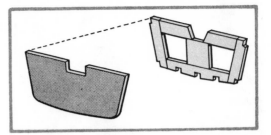

▲ Framing is fastened to plywood transom. Shown here is an outboard transom. Some designs use double thickness of plywood in the area where outboard motor is clamped.

▼ Two methods of joining framing members.

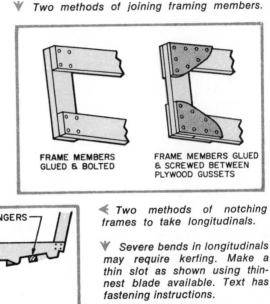

FRAME MEMBERS GLUED & BOLTED

FRAME MEMBERS GLUED & SCREWED BETWEEN PLYWOOD GUSSETS

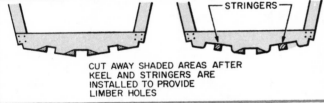

STRINGERS

CUT AWAY SHADED AREAS AFTER KEEL AND STRINGERS ARE INSTALLED TO PROVIDE LIMBER HOLES

◀ Two methods of notching frames to take longitudinals.

▼ Severe bends in longitudinals may require kerfing. Make a thin slot as shown using thinnest blade available. Text has fastening instructions.

▼ Below left: When fairing keel or other longitudinals, cut a notch in the keel at each frame, then fair between frames with a plane. Below right: The chines should be beveled to mate with the stem. To do this, spring chine into position so that it ends at the stem. Cut the bevel, using the stem as guide.

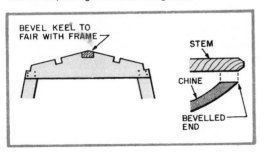

BEVEL KEEL TO FAIR WITH FRAME

STEM

CHINE

BEVELLED END

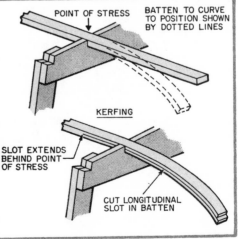

POINT OF STRESS

BATTEN TO CURVE TO POSITION SHOWN BY DOTTED LINES

KERFING

SLOT EXTENDS BEHIND POINT OF STRESS

CUT LONGITUDINAL SLOT IN BATTEN

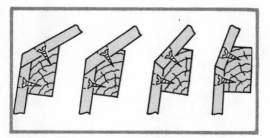

▲ *Example of changing bevel on chine between forward frame and stem. Beveling is easiest when chines are sprung on frames.*

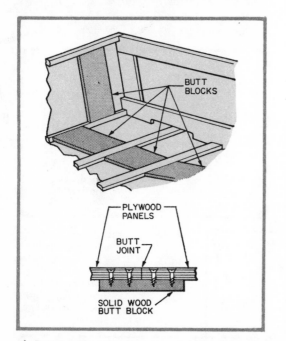

BUTT BLOCKS

PLYWOOD PANELS

BUTT JOINT

SOLID WOOD BUTT BLOCK

▲ *Butt blocks are used to reinforce joints in the hull planking. They should be installed between longitudinals and glued and screwed to planking. Joints in hull planking should be in-between transverse members, and in as flat an area as possible.*

cases the keel is perfectly straight and level, and its installation is no problem. It is set into its notches, glued and screwed into place at each frame, and screwed or bolted to the transom knee and stem. Be sure to countersink for all fastenings, as it is often necessary to level the keel to fair it with the frames.

Chines are installed next. Set them into their notches at the transom, and screw them in place. Then fasten them in place at each frame, working from one side of the boat to the other as you go forward to distribute the stress evenly. It may be necessary to use a wood rasp to fair the notches so the chines are usually beveled to fit flush against the stem.

Sheer clamps are installed in the same manner as the chines. At the forward ends, these may fasten to a bow plate that is part of the stem assembly. Finally, install stringers as required.

Where chines, clamps, or stringers must take a sharp bend, they may crack when you attempt to spring them into position. To prevent this, you can kerf them. Do not install a fastening through a kerfed section until the forward end of the member is clamped or fastened in place. Kerfing is often done to bottom stringers that extend forward for the foremost frame. Such stringers are fastened at the frame, *after* the bottom panels have been installed, by screws that go through the plywood and kerfed stringer into the frame.

All framing, including longitudinals, must be faired before side and bottom panels are installed. Use a long, thin, flexible batten to check for humps or ridges that must be trimmed. It is important that the plywood panels lie flush against the framing, so work slowly and carefully. Chines may need bevelling along their entire length, and almost always along the section between the forward frame and the stem. Cut limber holes alongside the keel and bottom stringers at each frame.

Treat all your framing with a good wood preservative. It's a good idea at this point, to paint these and any other areas that will not be accessible after the panels are in place.

Side and bottom panels. Normal plywood panels are 4 x 8 feet, although longer lengths usually can be obtained on special order. In most cases it is necessary to use more than one 8-foot length to make up each side and bottom panel; unless you can get sheets in longer lengths, you will need to butt sections together, with a backing block at the joint. Butt blocks should be of solid wood, at least 4 inches wide, and they should run the full distance between any longitudinals. Butt blocks can be installed after the panels are in place on the hull. Coat mating surfaces with glue, and run screws staggered about 2 inches apart through the plywood into the butt blocks.

If patterns are supplied for side and bottom panels, or if you make up patterns from scale drawings on the plans, trace the patterns on the plywood and cut out the pieces. Again, leave them slightly oversize to allow for trimming.

Sometimes it is necessary to clamp an uncut plywood panel to the framework, and mark the outline to be cut. When one panel is marked and cut, it can be used as a pattern for the matching panel on the opposite side of the boat.

When plywood must take a fairly severe curve (when clamping for marking, as above, or for final installation), it may be necessary to "steam" it to make it bend easily. Soak large rags, such as old towels, in boiling water, then drape them on the area to be bent. As the rags cool, replace them with hot ones. As the wood softens, it can be pulled down to the framework and clamped in place.

Install side panels first. Coat mating surfaces with glue and clamp the first panel in place. Use flat head wood screws and install them about 2 inches apart along chines, transom, sheer clamps, and bow. Drill pilot holes and countersink for each screw. At the transom, be sure to screw into the solid wood framing members, not into the plywood transom panel. Remove clamps, and trim the side panels flush with the transom, and with the chine as far forward as the foremost frame. Between this

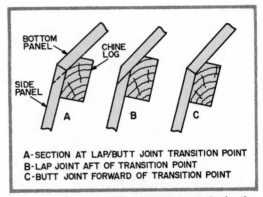

A-SECTION AT LAP/BUTT JOINT TRANSITION POINT
B-LAP JOINT AFT OF TRANSITION POINT
C-BUTT JOINT FORWARD OF TRANSITION POINT

▲ *A transition joint is used frequently in the forward portion of the hull planking. Bottom planking laps against the side in the aft portion of the joint. In the forward section, a butt joint is used. A transitional joint is not needed on flat or gradual vee bottom hulls.*

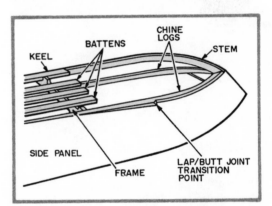

▲ *Location of the transition point is not critical, although it must be forward of the forward frame, as shown. The idea is to avoid exposing too much end grain of planking.*

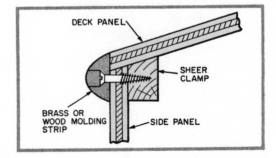

▲ *One common and easy method of protecting deck edges. Brass, wood or synthetic moldings are easily available, and easy to apply. Screws are countersunk and then plugged.*

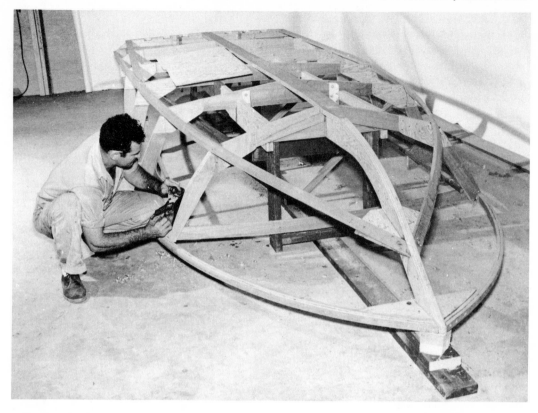

frame and the stem, trim the panel to provide a "transition joint." Aft of this joint, the bottom panel will lap over the edge of the side panel; forward of this joint, the edge of the bottom panel will butt against the edge of the side panel.

Where two or more sections of plywood are needed to make up each side panel, install butt blocks as outlined earlier.

Bottom panels are installed in the same manner as the side panels. Use a plane, wood rasp, or "Surform" type tool to trim them for a good butt joint along the centerline and at the stem. Trim them flush with the side panels aft of the transition joints.

Fiberglassing. If you plan to fiberglass the seams, the bottom, or the entire hull, this is the time to do it. Fiberglass tape over seams adds strength, and prevents moisture from entering the end grain of the plywood. As fiberglassing the entire bottom

adds to its strength, you can use thinner, easier-to-bend plywood bottom panels and still have the required strength. Fiberglassing the entire hull permits use of thinner side panels as well, and you can add color pigment to your final resin coat to eliminate the need for a paint job.

Before fiberglassing—or painting—cover all screw heads with wood putty. Sand the putty flush with the plywood after it has dried. If you do not use fiberglass, coat all exposed plywood edges with wood sealer to help prevent deterioration.

Turn the hull right side up. Block it carefully so that it has adequate support, and won't shift around as you work on the interior and topsides. Trim the side panels flush with the sheer clamps.

Now you can paint the interior of the hull. There will be areas that are impossible to see, and difficult to reach, after the boat is decked. Do not paint tops of frames, deck beams, sheer clamps, or other members to which glue must be applied later.

Interior woodwork. Install any interior battens, bulkheads, permanent floor board panels, engine stringers, or similar interior members. Again, paint anything you won't be able to see or reach later. Seats, lockers, berths, and cabinets are also easier to fit before the hull is decked.

Permanent fuel and water tanks, plumbing, control cables, and electric wiring should also be installed at this time, as well as the engine itself (if it is an inboard).

Decking. If your plans call for deck beams and carlines in addition to frame tops, cut these members to size and install them. Plywood deck panels can be cut using patterns to mark the stock, or by clamping the stock in place and marking the lines on it. Cut the stock slightly oversize, and trim the edges flush with the sides of the boat after installation.

To protect deck edges, coat them with a bedding compound and install a length of half-round wood or brass stock as a rub rail around the sheer line. Or you can use one of the ready-made plastic or synthetic rubber molding strips that are available at marine supply stores.

Superstructures. Windshields, coamings, even cabins are simple once you've finished the hull. Be sure all raw edges of plywood are sealed, and that any joints where fresh water might get trapped are well-protected and well-ventilated. This will prevent wood rot from getting a start.

Painting. Regular marine or exterior grade plywood should be coated with a surface sealer before painting to help prevent surface checking that could mar the appearance of the finish. Mahogany-faced plywood, often used for decking, should be filled and stained before it is varnished. Plastic-faced plywoods do not need surface sealers or prime coats.

For best results, at least two coats of paint are recommended—a primer and a finish coat, or two finish coats on plastic-faced plywood. You can use a matte (dull) finish paint for the first coat, and gloss or semi-gloss for the second.

If your boat is to be moored in salt water, or polluted fresh water, the bottom will need a coat of antifouling paint. This is true even if the bottom has been fiberglassed.

It's smart to use sealers, fillers, and primers made and recommended by the manufacturer of the finish paint you select. This insures proper paint adhesion and a longer trouble-free life for the entire paint system. For best results, be sure to follow the manufacturer's instructions!

Hardware. All exterior hardware should be set in bedding compound to prevent moisture from being trapped between fittings and the mounting surface. All hardware should be securely fastened—screws in plywood do *not* do the job. Use a solid wood backing block under the plywood, and screws that are long enough to get a good grip in the backing blocks. Hardware that is subject to any strain, such as cleats, chocks, bitts, and lifting rings should be *bolted* through the backing blocks, with generous washers between the nuts and the wood.

Some instructions given with plans for plywood boats will differ in particulars from information presented here. Often an individual boat will have requirements that cannot be covered in a general article such as this. In any case, follow the instructions given on *your* plans. This article covers normal, proven methods for plywood boat construction. If you have nothing to guide you but this article and a set of drawings (with proper measurements given), you can produce a boat of professional quality. And you will enjoy doing it.   T.B.

See also: ADHESIVES; BOAT BUILDING PROJECTS; BOATING: MAINTENANCE, BOAT; WOOD BENDING.

Build a
Buck Board

This light, easy-to-sail surf-board is simple to build

BUCK BOARD is an easy-to-build sailing surfboard that will give you hours of fun and excitement on lakes, bays, and other sheltered waterways. All you need are a few hand tools, simple materials, and a few hours of spare time in order to complete the job.

This boat is built to plans that are available along with full-size patterns. Patterns can be transferred to wood stock by punching along the lines with a sharp nail. Then use a pencil to connect the punch marks on the wood, and you're ready to cut out the parts.

Start with three frames, which are cut from ¼-inch plywood. Attach the 1 x 1-inch cleats to each for side members, keel, and deck batten. Note that no cleat is provided where the keel joins frame C, and that the cleats for the deck batten run the full width of the frames, in order to strengthen them.

The transom is made of an outer panel of ¼-inch plywood, and an inner member of ½-inch hardwood stock. The inner member is notched for the keel and deck batten, and it is cut smaller, around the edges, than the outer panel. This allows the side, deck, and bottom panels to lie flush with the outer edges of the plywood transom panel. Assemble the inner and outer sections with ¾-inch annular ring nails,

after coating the mating surfaces with glue. Space the nails about 3 inches apart, well-staggered.

The daggerboard trunk is assembled next. It also is made up of ¼-inch plywood and 1 x 1-inch cleats. One side of the trunk is a continuous member that extends the full distance between frames B and C; the other side of the trunk is just long enough to enclose the daggerboard. As in all other assembly steps, coat mating surfaces with glue. Nail the long side of the trunk to the three 1 x 1-inch vertical cleats, with a minimum of three ¾-inch nails per cleat. Next apply the upper and lower fore-and-aft cleats to the outboard side of the trunk in a similar manner, spacing nails about 4

Build a Buck Board

inches apart. The cleats are then assembled to the short side of the trunk. Attach the short side of the trunk to the large side with a minimum of three ¾-inch nails in each of the vertical cleats.

No building jig is needed for this boat, as assembly starts by mounting frames and transom on the 1 x 4-inch deck batten. Mark location of these units on the batten first, along with location of the daggerboard slot, and the bow block. Cut out the daggerboard slot; it should be equal to the width of the assembled daggerboard, with very little clearance. Mark and drill the hole for the mast step assembly.

Place the deck batten on a floor or workbench that is level, then mount the transom and frames in place. Make sure that each is square to the batten, and perpendicular to it. Fasten each with at least two 1½-inch screws at each member, after drilling pilot holes. Now mount the daggerboard trunk between frames B and C. Be sure that it is vertical, and centered on the deck batten centerline.

Make up the bow block, as shown on your plans, and install it at the forward end of the deck batten, then cut the batten to the shape of the bow block. Fair the bow block to allow the keel to be positioned between the side planking ends, and lie flush with the edges of the side planking.

The side planking is of ½-inch stock, with the ends left long for fitting. It is installed by starting at the bow and working aft, working from one side to the other to minimize distortion of the framework. Note that at the bow one side member overlaps the other, or the pieces may be butted together, and then the ends filed flat and covered with a wood or metal strip. Fasten the sides to all mating members with at least two 1¼-inch screws into each cleat, after coating matching surfaces with glue. Trim off the excess at the transom end.

The keel is a 1 x 4-inch member. Mark and cut out the daggerboard slot, then bevel the member. This step eliminates the need for fairing it later. It may be necessary to trim the frame notches slightly so the keel will lie flush and snug in each. Fasten with two 1½-inch screws at each cleat, after applying glue to the joints. Also glue and screw the keel to the centerboard trunk, using at least three 1½-inch #8 screws on each side.

SPECIFICATIONS

Length overall	11′11″
Beam	3′0″
Draft (board down)	2′10″
Sail area	66 sq. ft.
Weight	85 lbs.

Make up the mast step block, and install it with the mast step flange. The block is glued in place, and the flange is bolted through it.

Now the hull is ready for planking. Either the bottom or the deck may be done first. In each case it will be necessary to butt panels of plywood together to cover the entire length of the boat. These joints must be backed by butt blocks that extend the full width of each joint between the keel and side members, or deck batten and side members. The butt blocks also should extend at least 4 inches on each side of the joint. Glue the butt blocks in place, and fasten from the outside with ¾-inch nails or ⅝-inch #7 brass screws, spaced about 2 inches apart. Clinch over the protruding ends of nails, and peen or file flat protruding ends of screws.

The decking is cut from ¼-inch x 4 x 8-foot plywood panels, with the butt joint near the bow. Lay or clamp the panels in position, and mark around the outer extremities to provide your cutting line. Also mark for the daggerboard cutout, and mast step hole. Cut the panels slightly oversize to allow for trimming. Coat mating surfaces with glue, and fasten the panels to the boat with ¾-inch nails, spaced about 3 inches apart.

Bottom panels are installed in the same manner as the decking, but with a joint that runs the full length of the keel, and the butt joints at the aft end of the hull. Be sure to cut the slot for the daggerboard.

If you plan to fiberglass the boat, it can be done at this time.

With the hull right side up, install the mast step pipe. This is a 10-inch length of 2-inch galvanized pipe; it is screwed into the flange that is bolted to the mast step block. Make up a 2 x 6-inch diameter deck block, with a hole in its center, to secure the upper end of the pipe. Use an expansion bit to drill the hole, in order to get a snug fit. The deck block is secured to the deck with glue, and four 2-inch #10

At right of bench bulkheads A, B, C. Note: C has no cleat for keel. Finished transom at lower left of bench; two unassembled daggerboard trunk members above it.

screws, well countersunk, that reach into the deck batten. Now you can paint the hull, and mount hand rails, if desired.

The daggerboard is cut from 1-inch solid stock. A 1 x 1-inch cleat is screw fastened to one side of the daggerboard at the top; a ½ x 2-inch cap is then glued and screwed to the cleat. Make up the rudder in the same way; the tiller can be cut to a length you feel will be comfortable—about 48 inches is normal.

Mast and booms are of aluminum. Use 2-inch O.D. tubing with a .065-inch wall thickness for the mast, which is 10 feet 6 inches long, and 1½-inch O.D. tubing with a .049-inch wall thickness for the two booms. These are each 11 feet 8 inches long. The aluminum should be type 6061-T6, which is suitable for use in marine environment. Seal the ends of the tubes with cork or wood blocks so they will not sink if the boat is capsized.

Join the two booms at the forward ends with interlocking eye bolts. The eyes should be of the unwelded type, so one can be spread apart and hooked into the other, then closed again. The lower boom is at-

Build a Buck Board

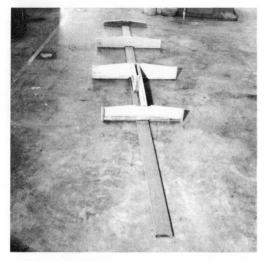

▲ This is how frame assembly looks with transom, bulkheads, daggerboard trunk in place. Slot for daggerboard has been cut in deck batten, hole for mast step drilled.

▲ Side planks and keel have been fastened in place, and the mast step block glued to keel. Note hole drilled for mast step plate bolt; a second bolt's in place.

▲ Half of the bottom planking is in place, with aft section positioned on the other side. Butt block extending from keel to side member is installed at this joint.

▲ Deck block, hand rails installed on hull. Note jam cleat on deck block. It might be necessary to ream inside of mast step at top, so tube can slide into place.

tached to the mast with an eye bolt and ring, as shown on the plans, or with a gooseneck fitting made specially for the lateen rig.

Attach all blocks, cleats, and eye straps with round head machine bolts that extend through both sides of the spars. File the nut end flush with the nut, and smooth as much as possible, to prevent snagging.

To make up the traveller for the sheet, install two eye straps, one on each side of the hull, about 12 inches forward of the transom. Run a length of ¼-inch line through one eye, and knot the end so that it will not pull through completely. Slip a bullet block onto the line, then run the line through the opposite eye, and knot that end so it cannot slip back through the eye. As an alternate, one end of the traveller line may be equipped with a harness snap for a quick-release.

Thread the sheet through the eye portion of the bullet block, and knot the end so it will not pull through. It is then run through the aft block on the boom, then the forward block. Normally, the sheet is hand-held, although a quick-action cam cleat could be installed along the centerline of the boat.

Secure the halyard to the eye bolt on the upper boom, then run the line through the block at the top of the mast, and down to the jam cleat at the base of the mast.

While it is possible to make up your own sails, it is best to go to a reputable sail-maker. The sails may be lashed to the booms with a line that runs through grommets in the sail, or the sail may be made with pockets that slide over the booms. The pocket, or "sock" for the upper boom runs the full length of the sail, and a hole must be left for the halyard eye strap.

For the lower boom, the pocket is just at the last 12 inches of the sail. The portion from this point forward is loose-footed; a line at the tack secures the sail at the boom junctions.

See also: ADHESIVES; BOATING; BOAT BUILDING; MAINTENANCE, BOAT.

MATERIALS LIST

Quantity	Size and Description		Purpose
2	¼"	4'x8' exterior or marine grade plywood	planking, decking, and bulkheads
1	¼"	4'x4' exterior or marine grade plywood	planking, decking, and bulkheads
	1"	1"x30' spruce or mahogany	frame and dagger-board cleats
2	½"	6"x13' spruce or mahogany	side planking
1	½"	4"x2' spruce or mahogany	transom
1	1"	4"x14' spruce or mahogany	keel and bow block
1	1"	4"x12' spruce or mahogany	deck batten
1	1"	12"x40" mahogany	daggerboard
1	1"	9"x40" mahogany	rudder
2	1"	1½"x6' mahogany	hand rails
1	2"x6" diameter fir or mahogany		deck block
as needed	#8	1¼" flathead wood screws	
as needed	#8	1½" flathead wood screws	
as needed	#10	2" flathead wood screws	
as needed	#14	¾" annular thread bronze nails	

NOTE: Also need, aluminum for mast and booms, sails, glue, cork, hardware and fittings.

PLANS: Glen L. Marine Designs, 9152 E. Rosecrans, Bellflower, Cal. 90706. Riggings and sail kits also available.

Other suppliers of kits and plans:
 Clark Craft, 16-4 Aqua Lane, Tonawanda, N.Y. 14150
 Craft Print Div., Boat Builder, 229 Park Ave. South, N.Y., N.Y. 10003

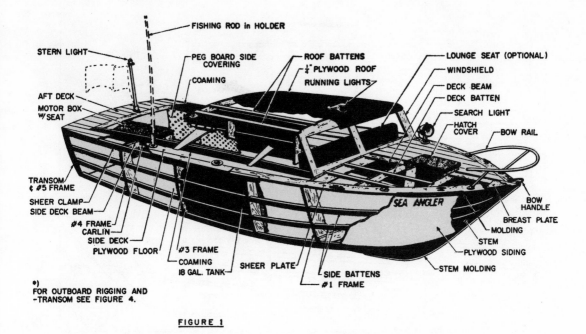

FISHING ROD in HOLDER

STERN LIGHT

PEG BOARD SIDE COVERING

COAMING

ROOF BATTENS
½" PLYWOOD ROOF
RUNNING LIGHTS

LOUNGE SEAT (OPTIONAL)
WINDSHIELD
DECK BEAM
DECK BATTEN
SEARCH LIGHT
HATCH COVER
BOW RAIL

AFT DECK
MOTOR BOX W/ SEAT

TRANSOM & #5 FRAME
SHEER CLAMP
SIDE DECK BEAM
#4 FRAME
CARLIN
SIDE DECK
PLYWOOD FLOOR
#3 FRAME
COAMING
18 GAL. TANK
SHEER PLATE
SIDE BATTENS
#1 FRAME

BOW HANDLE
BREAST PLATE
MOLDING
STEM
PLYWOOD SIDING
STEM MOLDING

SEA ANGLER

*) FOR OUTBOARD RIGGING AND
-TRANSOM SEE FIGURE 4.

FIGURE 1

Deep-vee Sea Angler

The top of this 20-footer can be permanent, removable, or folding canvas. She's constructed of plywood panels over hardwood frames and offers a variety of power options — 150 horses suggested for a cruising speed of 32 mph

SPECIFICATIONS

L.O.A.	20'
Beam	8'
Depth at stem	49"
Depth amidships	43"
Depth at transom	36"
Transom width	80"
Displacement	
Outboard	1700 lb.
Inboard	2200-2400 lb.
Draft	18"

SEA ANGLER is a 20-foot cruiser of the deep-vee hull type that has gained so much in popularity in recent years because of its ability to provide a high turn of speed with minimum pounding in rough seas. Actually, the concept of the deep vee is not new, but early attempts to produce hulls of this type were unsuccessful. At that time use of longitudinal steps, or lift rails, was

not understood, and the engines lacked the power needed for this type of hull.

For Sea Angler, an engine of about 150 hp is recommended, either as a straight inboard, an inboard/outboard, or a pair of outboards. This can give the boat a top speed of about 38 mph, and a cruising speed of about 32 mph. The flexibility of power options allows you to use an auto-

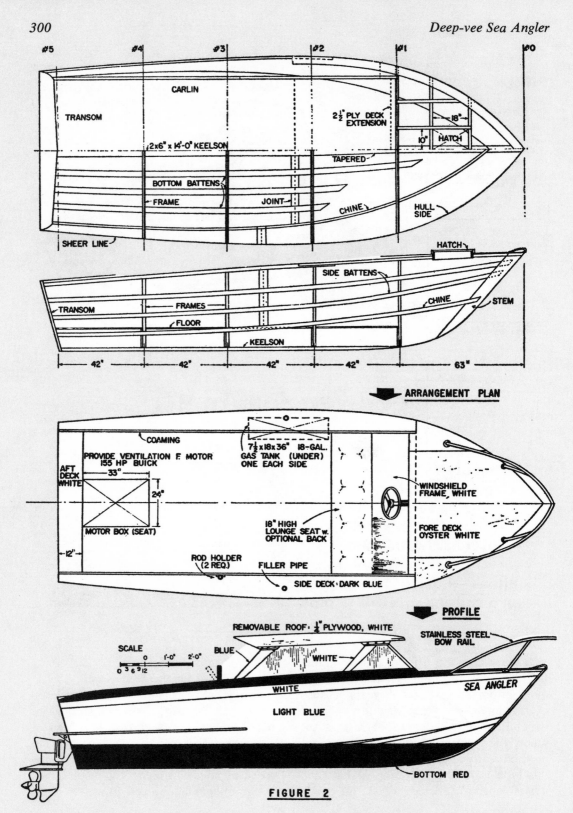

#5   #4   #3   #2   #1   #0

CARLIN

TRANSOM

2½" PLY DECK EXTENSION

18"

10"   HATCH

2x6" x 14'-0" KEELSON

TAPERED

BOTTOM BATTENS

FRAME   JOINT

CHINE

HULL SIDE

SHEER LINE

HATCH

SIDE BATTENS

TRANSOM   FRAMES

CHINE   STEM

FLOOR

KEELSON

42"   42"   42"   42"   63"

ARRANGEMENT PLAN

COAMING

7½ x18x 36" 18-GAL. GAS TANK (UNDER) ONE EACH SIDE

PROVIDE VENTILATION F. MOTOR 155 HP BUICK

33"

AFT DECK WHITE

24"

WINDSHIELD FRAME, WHITE

MOTOR BOX (SEAT)

18" HIGH LOUNGE SEAT w. OPTIONAL BACK

FORE DECK OYSTER WHITE

12"

ROD HOLDER (2 REQ.)   FILLER PIPE

SIDE DECK DARK BLUE

PROFILE

REMOVABLE ROOF ½" PLYWOOD, WHITE

STAINLESS STEEL BOW RAIL

SCALE

0   1'-0"   2'-0"

0 3 6 9 12

BLUE

WHITE

WHITE

SEA ANGLER

LIGHT BLUE

BOTTOM RED

FIGURE 2

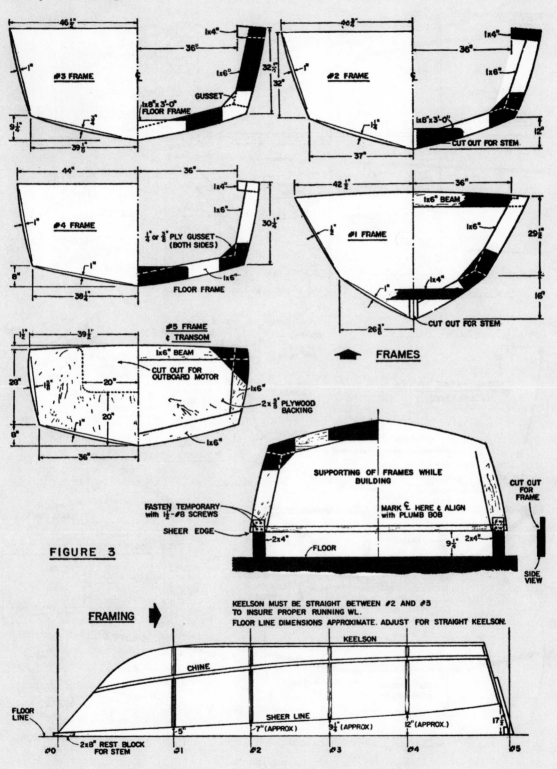

FIGURE 3

FRAMES

FRAMING

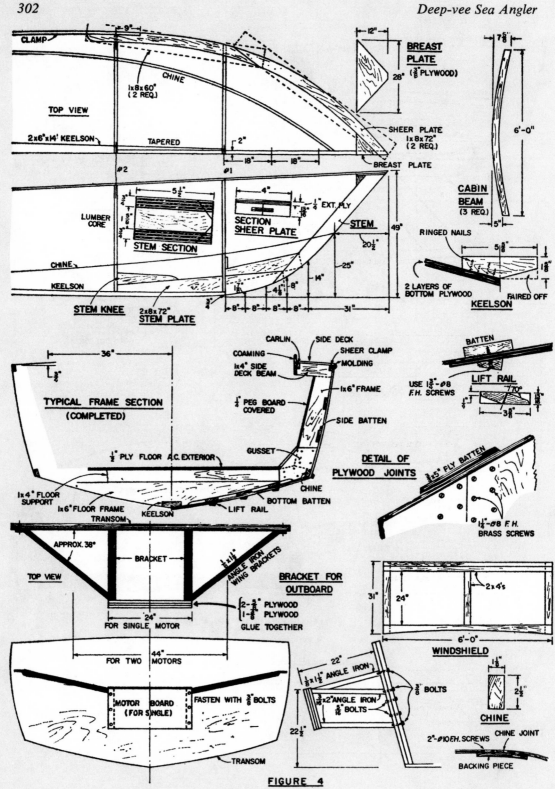

FIGURE 4

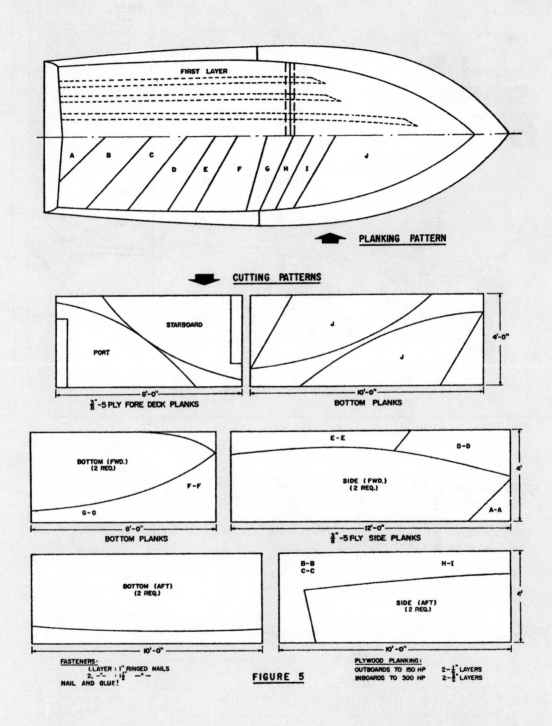

FIRST LAYER

A B C D E F G H I J

PLANKING PATTERN

CUTTING PATTERNS

STARBOARD

PORT

3/8"-5 PLY FORE DECK PLANKS
— 8'-0" —

J

J

4'-0"

BOTTOM PLANKS
— 10'-0" —

BOTTOM (FWD.)
(2 REQ.)

F-F

G-G

BOTTOM PLANKS
— 6'-0" —

E-E

D-D

SIDE (FWD.)
(2 REQ.)

A-A

4'

3/8"-5 PLY SIDE PLANKS
— 12'-0" —

BOTTOM (AFT)
(2 REQ.)

— 10'-0" —

B-B
C-C

H-I

SIDE (AFT)
(2 REQ.)

4'

— 10'-0" —

FASTENERS:
1. LAYER : 1" RINGED NAILS
2. —"— : 1½" —"—
NAIL AND GLUE!

FIGURE 5

PLYWOOD PLANKING:
OUTBOARDS TO 150 HP   2-¼" LAYERS
INBOARDS TO 300 HP   2-⅜" LAYERS

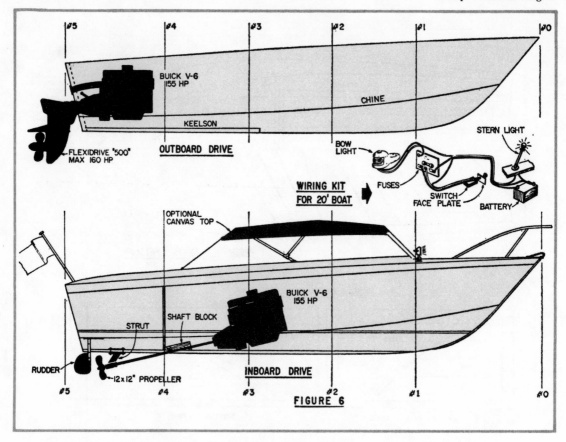

FIGURE 6

MATERIALS LIST		
Quantity	**Size and Description**	**Purpose**
2	⅝″ 5½″x16′ hardwood of your choice (see text)	coamings
1	³/₄″ 1½″x12′ hardwood of your choice (see text)	outer keel
8	1″ 4″x8′ hardwood of your choice (see text)	floor beams and deck battens
4	1″ 4″x10′ hardwood of your choice (see text)	side battens
6	1″ 4″x12′ hardwood of your choice (see text)	sheer clamps and bottom battens
6	1″ 4″x14′ hardwood of your choice (see text)	floor longerons
6	1″ 4″x16′ hardwood of your choice (see text)	bottom battens, carlins and lift rails

Quantity	Size and Description	Purpose
10	1″ 6″x8′ hardwood of your choice (see text)	deck beams and frame
2	1″ 6″x12′ hardwood of your choice (see text)	frame
5	1″ 8″x10′ hardwood of your choice (see text)	deck plates and frame
2	1″ 8″x14′ hardwood of your choice (see text)	deck plates
2	1¼″ 2½″x6′ hardwood of your choice (see text)	chines
2	1¼″ 2½″x14′ hardwood of your choice (see text)	chines
1	2″ 4″x12′ hardwood of your choice (see text)	spray rails
1	2″ 6″x6′ hardwood of your choice (see text)	stem
1	2″ 6″x14′ hardwood of your choice (see text)	keelson
1	2″ 8″x6′ hardwood of your choice (see text)	stem
4	⅜″ 4′x10′ exterior plywood	hull sides and deck
2	⅜″ 4′x12′ exterior plywood	hull sides and deck
4	⅜″ 4″x8′ exterior plywood	hull sides and deck
1	¼″ 4″x8′ exterior plywood	hull sides and deck
2	⅝″ 4′x7′ exterior plywood (use doubled)	hull sides and deck
1	¾″ 4′x8′ exterior plywood	hull sides and deck
as needed	#8 1¼″ flathead screws	planking
as needed	#10 2″ flathead screws	battens
as needed	#12 3″ flathead screws	keel
as needed	#12 2½″ flathead screws	chines
5 lbs.	1¼″ serrated nails, double dipped zinc, Monel or bronze	
2 gals.	Resorcinal glue	double planking
5	#177 1¼″x10′ aluminum boat molding	
5 yards	54″ Nautolex	deck covering
as needed	#88 Nautolex adhesive	deck covering
12 yards	50″ heavy duty fiberglass cloth	bottom
5 gals.	resin	bottom

NOTE: Also need, paint, engine(s), trim, seats, windshield, etc.

PLANS: Craft Print Div., Boat Builder, 229 Park Ave. So., N.Y., N.Y. 10003

Other suppliers of kits and plans:
  Luger Industries, 3800 W. Highway 13, Burnsville, Minn. 55378
  Bruce Roberts Boat Plans, 19530 Lenaire Dr., Miami, Fla. 31571
  Glen L. Marine Designs, 9152 Rosecrans, Bellflower, Cal. 90706
  Samson Marine Design, Ltd., 833 River Rd., Richmond, B.C., Canada

motive conversion of your own choice, in addition to stock marine engines.

Construction is of plywood panels over hardwood frames, which makes the job simple for anyone familiar with the use of common hand tools. White oak is the best frame material but good, clear white oak may be hard to get. You can also use Douglas fir, or mahogany. The new plastic-coated plywoods are ideal for hull sides and decks. The surface takes an exceptionally smooth paint finish with long-lasting qualities. For the bottom, which is "double planked," use two thicknesses of AC or AB grade exterior plywood. Bond the B or C sides together. A layer of fiberglass on the bottom is recommended.

If possible, build the boat indoors, in a garage or shed, but be sure you have plenty of working room: at least 24 x 12 feet is recommended, with overhead clearance of 10 feet.

First, draw full size patterns of the frames, stem, and sheer plates on building paper, using the dimensions shown in Fig. 3 and Fig. 4. Transfer the lines from paper to the wood stock with a dressmaker's toothed wheel. At this time you can also make your patterns for the other structural members shown in Fig. 4, and for the plywood panels, as shown in Fig. 5.

Cut out the frame members, and assemble the frames with plywood gussets glued and nailed or screwed to the frames, as shown in Fig. 3. Make up the stem assembly, as shown in Fig. 4, and be sure that it is mortised between frame #1 and frame #2 to take the keelson.

Fasten lengths of 2 x 4 to each frame so that when the frames are in position, upside down on the floor, the keelson will lie absolutely straight in its notches. The dimensions given for the extension shown in Fig. 3 are approximate, as you must take imperfections in the floor into consideration. If necessary, you can use shims under the extensions to get the correct alignment. Note

that 2 x 2 crosspieces are attached between the sides of frames #2, #3, and #4, to prevent any misalignment during construction.

Notch each frame for the keelson, and notch partially for the chines, sheer clamps, and side battens. These notches will be completed, as work progresses, by running a hand saw alongside the longitudinal member as it's held in position. Notch #1 frame for the bottom batten closest to the keel, on each side. A single notch, almost the full width of each bottom half, is used for the three bottom battens on the remaining frames as shown on Fig. 4.

Make up the keelson from a 14-foot length of 2 x 6. Taper it between frame #2 and frame #1, as shown in Fig. 2. Cut out the transom from two pieces of $\frac{5}{8}$-inch plywood. Glue and screw them together, and glue and screw the plywood lamination to frame #5. Use large clamps to hold the assembly while the glue is setting.

Set up the transom, frames, and stem in position, and align them. Install the keelson, fastening it to each frame with 3-inch #12 flathead screws. Be sure to countersink the screws at #1 frame quite deep, as the keelson must be faired in to the stem piece. Use resorcinol glue on all mating surfaces before putting in the fastenings.

Bevel the forward ends of the chines so they will fit flush against the stem, and fasten them to the stem with 2½-inch #12 screws. Work aft, one frame at a time, and install the chines to the frames with 2½-inch #12 screws after cutting each notch so the chines fit flush with the outer edges of the frame. Install the sheer clamps, side battens, and bottom battens in the same manner. The transom can be notched clear through for all longitudinals, which are trimmed flush with the transom, and the entire assembly then fiberglassed.

Cut the large plywood pieces for the inner bottom "planking," and install in place. Provide butt blocks, as shown in Fig. 4,

Deep-vee Sea Angler

that extend the full distance between bottom battens (see Fig. 2). Cut out the small plywood pieces that make up the outer skin. It's a good idea to lightly tack these outer pieces in place before applying glue to make sure all joints are trimmed to provide clean, snug joints. Apply a liberal coat of glue to all mating surfaces, and screw the outer layer of plywood to the inner layer. Sand the bottom so that there are no ridges at the joints, and cover with fiberglass.

Make up the lift rails as shown in Fig. 4. Use 16-foot lengths of 1 x 4, cut in half as illustrated. The lift rails are cut the same length as the bottom battens to which they are attached.

The sides are a single layer of plywood, and the panels are installed in the same manner as the inner bottom panels.

Turn the hull right side up, and remove the lengths of 2 x 4 that were used to hold the frames in position. You can paint the interior of the hull at this time, or at least those portions that will be hard to reach after the decking is in place.

Decking can be made of ⅜-inch plywood, but ½-inch exterior grade is recommended for added strength. You can use AC grade exterior plywood, with the C side down. Cover the decks with a good vinyl-supported fabric, such as Nautolex, for a long-lasting, good-looking surface.

Install the engine, as shown in Fig. 6, and add the cockpit trim and seats. You can make your own windshield, as shown in Fig. 4, or buy a ready-made unit. If you make your own, use Plexiglas or a shatterproof safety glass. Do not use regular window glass.

The top can be made up as a permanent unit, or you can use a removable hard top, or a folding canvas top. Details are illustrated in Fig. 1, Fig. 2, Fig. 4, and Fig. 6.

See also: BOATING; BOAT BUILDING; MAINTENANCE, BOAT.

Build an Islander

This kit-built, trailerable family cruiser can save you up to $2,500 or more over the cost of a ready-made boat

ISLANDER is a fiberglass family cruiser designed for outboard or stern drive power. It sleeps two in full-length forward vee-bunks, and a folding dinette table converts to an additional two-sleeper bunk. There's an enclosed head, a galley, and a roomy cockpit—all in a 20-foot rig that's easily trailered to your favorite waterway.

Finally, this is a boat you can build yourself, at a saving of hundreds of dollars over a comparable factory-built model. And don't let the fiberglass construction scare you; a kit provides modular units that are assembled with no muss, no fuss! About the only tools needed are a screwdriver and a paint brush. Even the building jig is made up from the shipping crate itself, and the average garage provides plenty of room for the boat's construction.

This little cruiser will take stern drive engine packages up to 220 hp, in complete kits that also are available. Those of 110 hp or 130 hp are recommended for good performance under normal conditions. If you want to use outboard power, you can mount your engine on a special bracket be-

hind the transom, or make a standard transom cut-out. A self-bailing motor well is supplied that fits between divided rear seats.

To begin, assemble the lower hull reinforcing members. These are pre-cut, interlocking panels of ¾-inch marine plywood. Brass screws are provided for fastenings, but you may wish to use galvanized or Everdure fittings if the boat will be operated in salt water.

Make up the building jig, and support the assembled bottom framework on the jig. Lower the fiberglass bottom right over this framework, then slip the molded side sections into place. Interlocking flanges on the sections eliminate any guesswork, and they hold the pieces in place until stainless steel screws, furnished with the kit, are installed through the flanges.

Next, install the transom section in the same manner.

Now make up a cradle for the hull, again using material from the shipping container. Turn the boat right side up, and onto this cradle. The next step is to bond everything in place from the inside, using strips of fiberglass embedded in resin.

Work along one seam or joint at a time, and apply a band of resin slightly wider than the fiberglass strip. Work resin into a fiberglass matt strip, saturating it well, then place the strip into position in the boat. You must be sure that the resin in the

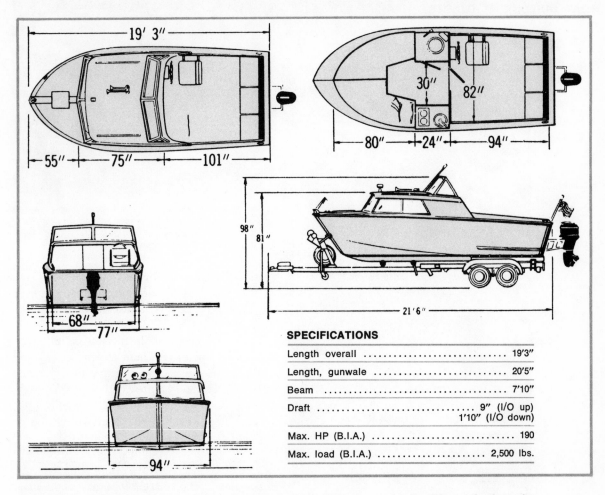

SPECIFICATIONS

Length overall	19'3"
Length, gunwale	20'5"
Beam	7'10"
Draft .... 9" (I/O up)	
1'10" (I/O down)	
Max. HP (B.I.A.)	190
Max. load (B.I.A.) .... 2,500 lbs.	

matt makes good contact with the resin applied along the seam or joint. Be sure there are no "voids," air pockets between the matt and the hull.

As the resin sets up fairly quickly, just mix enough to do one small section at a time. It's a good idea to buy a supply of disposable plastic gloves, and to wear the oldest clothes you have. Once resin gets on anything, it never comes off.

Next, the fiberglass deck is lowered into place, and fastened with stainless steel screws. Bond the joint on the inside with resin and fiberglass cloth. Install the ¾-inch marine plywood side reinforcing members, and bond them in place.

At this point, the basic hull is complete. This is the time to install your engine, if you are using the inboard/outboard package, as well as fuel tanks, fuel lines, elec-

trical wiring, and plumbing whether the boat will be inboard or outboard powered. These items are much easier to install before the cabin and cabin top are in place.

When this interior work is finished, add the after cabin bulkhead, cabin sides, and windshield. All parts are complete; you need only fasten them in place with the screws provided. The cabin top is a single molded unit that is lowered into place and fastened.

Now you can add the finishing touches to the cabin interior and the cockpit: bunks, dinette table, cabinets, flooring, helm control station.

Finally, install all the deck hardware, trim items, and such options as the "flying bridge" windshield. Note that one of the options is a foam flotation kit, and its use is recommended to provide 2400 pounds of

 *Assembling lower hull reinforcing. Pre-cut
3/4" interlocking marine plywood, solid oak
panels are used. Brass screws included in kit.*

*Lowering fiberglass deck into place, fasten
with stainless steel screws. Bond inside joint
with resin, fiberglass. Install 3/4" side reinforcing members, bond.*

*Slipping the molded transom into place.
Interlocking joints of transom mate with corresponding flanges of bottom, side sections.
Using stainless steel screws, fiberglass pieces
are fastened together.*

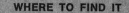 *Installing cabin top. Lower one-piece mold-
ed fiberglass cabin top into place, fasten. Next
complete cabin, cockpit interior, accessories.*

*Fiberglass bond joints, seams, hull rein-
forcement. Fiberglass matt strips are saturated
with resin and are then placed over joints,
seams between molded sections.*

positive flotation, more than enough to support the hull if it is swamped.

Now all that's needed is to load the boat
aboard a trailer, and it's ready for launch-
ing. Even the trailer is available as a kit.

See also: BOATING; BOAT BUILDING; MAINTENANCE,
BOAT; HULLS.

WHERE TO FIND IT

The Islander Kit is available from Luger Indus-
tries, 3800 W. Highway 13, Burnsville, Minn. 55378.
Other suppliers of boat kits and plans include
Bruce Roberts Boat Plans, 19530 Lenaire Dr.,
Miami, Fla. 31571; Glen L. Marine Designs, 9152
Rosecrans, Bellflower, Cal. 90706; Clark Craft,
16-4 Aqua Lane, Tonawanda, N. Y. 14150; and
Craft Print Div., Boat Builder, 229 Park Ave. So.,
N. Y., N. Y. 10003.

Spark of Life for Your Engine

Know your engine's ignition system and increase your boat's available power; this knowledge could be a lifesaver if your engine stalls off-shore

IF YOU OWN A BOAT, you ought to be able to check out and correct troubles in your ignition. Caught in a blow offshore, your ability to repair a conked-out system could save your life. Furthermore, ignition systems do wear out with age and use. If you want satisfactory engine performance, periodic maintenance is a must.

Satisfactory engine performance depends upon "teamwork" on the part of all ignition components. The way these ignition components work, and their relation to each other often confuses the average boatman when he attempts to check out ignition troubles. In order to locate and correct ignition problems quickly, the boatman should thoroughly understand the function of each ignition unit and its relation to the other units.

The ignition system and how it works. A complete study of the operation of the system is beyond the scope of this article. Basically, the ignition system consists of two functional sections:

1. Low-Voltage Section—converts the low-voltage direct current delivered by the battery to high secondary voltage by means of the ignition coil.

2. High-Voltage Section—supplies the high-voltage pulses by means of the distributor and the spark plug wires to each combustion chamber at the precise moment for proper ignition of the fuel-air mixture.

The battery is the basic source of energy for the ignition system. When the ignition switch is turned on, primary current flows in the primary circuit. When the breaker points in the distributor are closed, current flows in the primary winding of the ignition coil, then through the breaker points to ground, and back to the grounded terminal of the battery. The current flowing in the primary winding builds up a magnetic field that surrounds both the primary and secondary windings.

When the breaker points open, the flow of current in the primary winding is cut off. Instantly the magnetic field snaps back, and this surge induces a high voltage in the secondary winding. A condenser connected across the breaker points prevents arcing and consequent burning of the contacts, and speeds up the collapse of the magnetic field.

The high voltage is fed to the distributor rotor and to the proper spark plug at the precise instant required.

The 12-volt ignition system. The 12-volt ignition system was designed to provide the higher ignition voltages required by the modern high-compression marine engines, to provide a higher generator output to supply the host of electrical accessories aboard today's boats, and to provide more cranking power for the larger, high-compression engines.

By combining a ballast resistor in series with the ignition coil primary winding, the

boat, fiberglass: see boat building projects

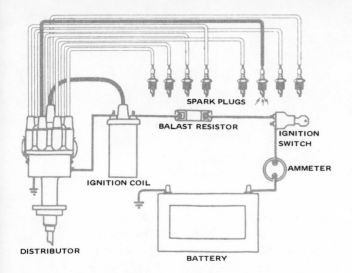

The principal components of an engine ignition system.

efficiency of the 12-volt system was vastly improved. The ballast resistor consists of a special alloy wire that has a positive temperature coefficient. That is, the resistance of the wire increases with heat. A large amount of current can flow through the wire when it is cold, but only a small amount when it is hot. At low speeds, when the breaker points are closed longer, the ballast resistor heats up, its resistance increases, and the current flowing through the breaker points and the primary of the ignition coil is limited to safe values. At higher speeds, when the breaker points remain closed a very short time, the ballast resistor cools off, lowers its resistance and allows more current to flow in the primary winding so that the magnetic field can build up faster.

Spark plugs and ignition. Our illustrations show graphically typical voltages required to fire the spark plugs over the engine rpm range, together with the voltage available from an ignition system in good condition. The decrease in available voltage as engine rpm is increased occurs because the breaker points are closed for a shorter time and the current flowing in the primary winding is cut off before the maximum magnetic field can be established.

Any deficiency in the primary circuit that may reduce the current flowing in the primary winding will reduce the voltage available at the spark plug. Any deficiency in the secondary circuit will increase the voltage required. In either case, misfiring generally results. For example, in the primary circuit, any point of high resistance, such as loose connections or burned breaker points, will reduce the current flowing in the primary winding so that a drop in spark plug voltage will result. Losses in the secondary circuit, such as poor connections in the coil or distributor towers, dirty distributor cap, or defective spark plug cables, will also result in a loss of voltage available at the spark plugs.

Misfiring due to a defective ignition system can often be corrected by installing new spark plugs, since the voltage required by new plugs is lower than that required by used plugs. But unless the ignition system malfunction is corrected, the misfiring condition will soon return.

Fouled spark plugs short-circuit the ignition system and reduce the available voltage. Worn plugs increase the voltage required because of the wider gap and rounded electrodes. Plugs properly gapped, with sharp edges on the electrodes, fire at a much lower voltage. Plugs eroded to the extent that proper gap cannot be obtained should be given the deep six. Never save an old plug for a spare. A *new* plug can prevent a headache.

Servicing the system. Periodic maintenance of the ignition system is required to ensure satisfactory engine operation. The objective of ignition service is to keep the available voltage as high as possible and the required voltage as low as possible.

The choice of replacement parts is important if optimum performance is to be achieved. Original service parts are your best bet in meeting these requirements.

The distributor. The distributor cap should be removed and wiped clean with a dry cloth. Make a visual inspection for cracks, carbon tracks, and corroded high-voltage terminals and if any of these are discovered, install a new distributor cap. If the cap is replaced, be sure that the spark plug cables are installed in the same towers from which they were removed and that they are forced firmly down into place.

If the inserts inside the distributor cap are burned excessively the cap should be replaced. (However, the vertical face of the insert will show some evidence of burning in normal operation.) Check the inserts for signs of mechanical interference with the rotor tip.

The carbon brush and spring in the center of the cap should be checked to ensure that the brush moves freely in the cap and that the spring is not burned or corroded. Be sure that the graphite tip on the brush is intact. If necessary, replace the brush and spring.

Check the rotor for cracks and inspect the blade for excessive burning. Replace if necessary, but be sure to obtain the correct rotor. Never file the end of the rotor blade as this increases the air gap between the rotor and distributor cap tower inserts and will cause excessive arcing and electrical erosion.

Breaker point contacts can be inspected without removing the distributor from the engine. A small dental mirror is handy in making this check. Some pitting of one contact, with a corresponding build-up on the opposite contact is normal, after the breaker points have been in service. If they show a frosty gray color and are not badly pitted, leave them alone. *Never attempt to file or clean used contacts.* If the contacts are burned black, or blue-black, or if they are badly pitted, the distributor should be removed from the engine for replacement of the breaker points and for further examination.

When you remove the distributor from the engine, the position of the distributor base in relation to the engine block should

be marked and the position of the rotor noted so that the distributor may be properly reinstalled. Although it's possible in many cases to install contacts without removing the distributor, it's not recommended. It's quite easy to remove and replace the distributor, and having it off the engine makes it more accessible and gives you a chance to clean all the parts and check them for wear.

If you install new breaker points, be sure the contact surfaces are properly aligned. Preassembled contacts should not require alignment if the breaker arm spring is pushed down firmly on the attaching screw. When it is necessary to align contacts, bend only the stationary contact support. DON'T BEND THE BREAKER ARM!

The contact gap should be checked with a round wire feeler gauge. Consult your engine manual to determine the proper gap, but if you don't have a manual, set the gap to .020-inch (twenty-thousandths). After adjusting the gap tighten the locking screw and recheck. *When adjusting contact spacing, be sure the rubbing block is on the highest point of the cam.*

When installed, the contacts should be cleaned with a few drops of lighter fluid on

▼ *Why you can't reach maximum speed. As shown on the chart, when engine speed rises above 3,000 rpm, the voltage available from a poorly maintained ignition system drops below the amount required by used spark plugs. That means that under these circumstances, your engine can't reach its maximum rpm.*

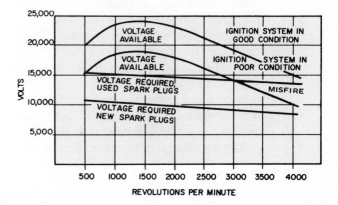

linen tape. Then pull a strip of clean, dry tape through the contacts to remove residue. *This is a very important step as the presence of oil, grease, or dirt on the contact surfaces is by far the greatest cause of contact failure.*

Lubrication should be used sparingly within the distributor as excessive oil or grease on the cam, breaker plate, breaker arm pivot, or on the felt wick in the top of the cam will get on the contacts and cause rapid burning and consequent failure. In addition to a light film of high-temperature grease on the cam lobes, and one drop of oil on the breaker arm pivot, add three drops of medium weight oil to the felt wick in the top of the cam, and a light film of high-temperature grease to the breaker plate pivots. Add five drops of medium weight engine oil to the oiler on the outside of the distributor case.

Centrifugal spark advance is accomplished by weights that swing outward by centrifugal force as the distributor shaft rotates. Sticking weights, due to broken or stretched springs, can cause poor acceleration, loss of top speed, and detonation that can quickly damage your engine. Here's how to spot check centrifugal advance:

Grip the distributor shaft or the rotor between thumb and forefinger and *twist in the direction of rotation.* On release, the rotor or shaft should snap back to its original position. If it returns slowly or not at all, you need new springs.

The ignition wiring. The ignition wiring consists of a primary low-voltage circuit and a secondary high-voltage circuit. Since the primary operates with low voltage, it must have low electrical resistance. Tight, corrosion-free connections, including battery connections, are important to satisfactory ignition performance. Check the wiring in the primary circuit carefully for loose connections, damaged and oil-soaked insulation and broken wire strands.

The secondary circuit operates on high voltage, requiring good insulation of spark plug cables and other components of the system. Many cases of spark plug misfiring have been traced to the spark plug cables. Here's a simple way you can check the insulation of spark plug cables and distributor cap boots. No elaborate test equipment is required, and it takes only a few minutes to do. Here's how it works:

You'll need a length of wire with an alligator clip on each end. Attach one clip to a good engine ground, then clip the other end to a screwdriver shank to use as a probe. Remove one spark plug cable and start the engine. With the engine running, probe around the ignition coil high-voltage cable—the one that goes to the center tower of the distributor—and its boot. If you see any sparks jumping from the coil boot or cable, both the boot and the cable should be replaced.

Next, with the engine still running, probe around the disconnected plug cable and boot. If you see any sparks, replace the whole set of spark plug cables and boots. If no sparks are seen, reconnect that cable and proceed to the next one. If any one of the spark plug cables or boots reveal sparks, you should replace the entire set.

Timing. Whenever breaker points are replaced, the timing should be reset to the engine manufacturer's specifications. You are strongly advised to have this done by a competent mechanic who uses a timing light. Advancing the distributor until a ping is heard, then backing off until the ping disappears is asking for trouble, especially on high-speed, high-compression engines, as such adjustments can result in over-heated and burned spark plugs, detonation, and serious damage to the engine.

Learn the simple checks and adjustments yourself, however, and you'll be able to trouble-shoot offshore if the need should ever come.   L.H.

See also: BATTERIES; EMERGENCY BOAT REPAIRS; IGNITION SYSTEM, AUTO.